BEYOND THE MEMORIAL

The Stories of the Titchfield men who fought in World War One

Amanda Laws

Exhibition researchers: Richard Boden, Louise Bullivant, Phil Burner, Dawne Dunton and Amanda Laws

Published by Honeybee Books
Broadoak, Dorset
www.honeybeebooks.co.uk

Copyright © Amanda Laws 2016
Cover Design by Phil Burner

The right of Amanda Laws to be identified as the author of this work has been asserted by her in accordance with the Copyright, Designs and Patents Act 1988.

No part of this book may be reproduced in any form or by any electronic or mechanical means including information storage and retrieval systems without permission in writing from the author.

Printed in the UK using paper from sustainable sources

ISBN: 978-1-910616-58-1

Profits from the sale of this book go to the Royal British Legion

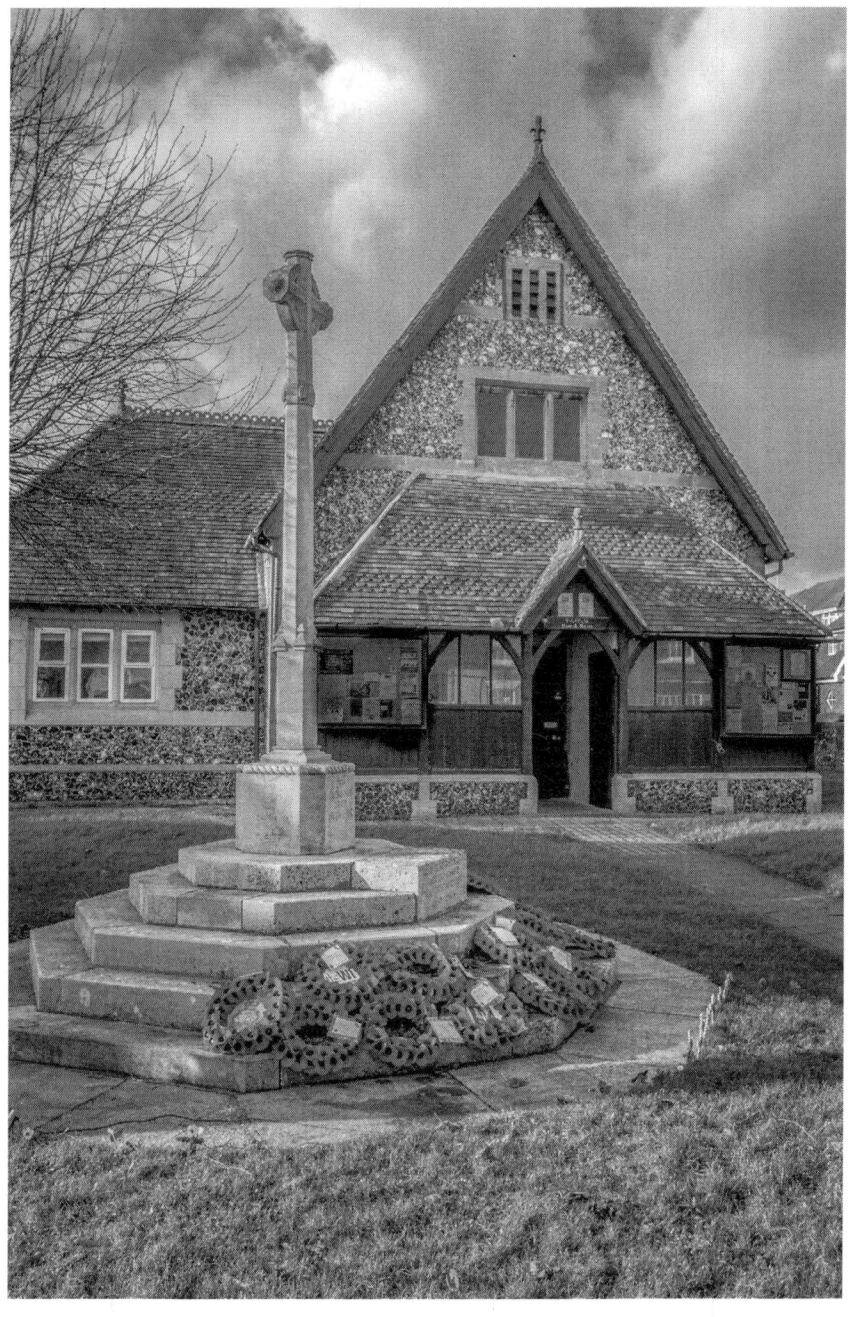

Titchfield Remembers Project

Foreword

The long list of names on the village War Memorial, of Titchfield men who fell in the Great War, is a sombre reminder of the devastating impact such huge losses had here and in other local communities across the nation. But as generations pass and memories fade, the backgrounds of those who volunteered, or were conscripted, are becoming forgotten.

So the people of Titchfield now have special cause to be grateful to Amanda Laws, and her researchers, for this sensitively composed and well-illustrated account of the different and poignant stories that lie behind each name of the men from Titchfield who paid the supreme sacrifice.

Here in these pages we learn about their individual lives before they went off to the Front - never to return. There are references to some who did come back safely, having survived horrific experiences, but often with their health severely weakened. We read of a family who not only lost two boys in action, but also three more who, shortly after returning home, died from the 'flu epidemic.

Thanks to this book, local people, and visitors to the Titchfield Memorial, will be able to discover the human stories beyond each inscription, to ponder the huge sacrifice of the men of this village – and to be quietly thankful for the peace and freedom that, to the great cost of the lives of others before us, can still be enjoyed in this ancient place today.

Vice Admiral Peter Wilkinson CB, CVO
National President, The Royal British Legion

Titchfield Remembers Exhibition 3rd August 2014 Titchfield Parish Rooms, with members of TACT reading 'Letters from Home'

Preface

In 2013 I looked at the names on the Titchfield War Memorial from the Great War and wondered about these men, their families and their lives before 1914. It seemed that other residents in the village had been thinking too, so we got together and looked 'beyond the memorial' to gather their stories.

At the same time I decided to look at the records of other deceased men who were born within the ecclesiastical parish of Titchfield, which included Locksheath before 1893. I wanted to ensure that each man had been included on a memorial somewhere. I found that some were not commemorated anywhere and others were honoured in more than one place.

Nine additional names came from that research and it was these and the original 41 men that formed the backbone of an exhibition that was held in the Parish Rooms in Titchfield on the eve of the anniversary of the declaration of war on August 3rd 2014 with funding from the local theatre group TACT. The objective was to expand our knowledge by gathering personal stories from living relatives still in the village and beyond. The success of the day was a delightful surprise with relatives coming from far and wide to give us more information. We were also interested in stories of the men who survived and so their relatives were welcomed too. After that day sections of the exhibition were put up in various local venues followed by commemoration windows being designed by residents for the village carnival.

The reading of the names at the church service on the 11th November 2014 was poignant, as for the first time we had a face or a story to put to the name.

In 2015 funding was secured to write this book.

Acknowledgements

The encouragement from Titchfield residents and our families, evident at the exhibition in 2014 was much appreciated and provided the impetus to complete this project. I am also extremely grateful for the information, photographs and support offered by all the Titchfield families and relatives of the servicemen, which has enabled this book to become something special.

Titchfield Remembers April 2016

Team from left Phil Burner, Dawne Dunton, Amanda Laws, Richard Boden & Louise Bullivant (Image K Laws)

Contributors

Funding - Titchfield Arts Community Theatre (exhibition),

Exhibition Actors - Alison Ascough, Annette DeVoil, Jack Fitt

Exhibition transport - Ian McGuire

The Royal British Legion

The Royal Naval Benevelent Fund

Carnival windows 2014 - Titchfield Bonfire Boys & residents

Titchfield Parish News - Brian Patten

Members of the Titchfield History Society

Funding - Fareham Community Action Trust (book)

Hampshire War Memorials - Steve Jarvis

Cranleigh War Memorial Project - Rod Weale

Contributers to The Great War Forum

National Archives research - Chris Jones -

Early village images - Peter Noyce ,Geoff Piper, Michael Prior

Thiepval images - Pam & Ken Linge

Gallipoli images – Geoff Allan (I.O.W. Family History Society)

The War Graves Photographic Project (TWGPP)

Hampshire War Memorials - David Adams

Members of Titchfield Nostalgia Facebook page

Editing & proofreading – Kim Laws, Louise Bullivant & family

All contemporary images (unless indicated) – Phil Burner

A Trip to France

On Monday 17th August 2015 I went to Northern France with photographer Phil Burner and our partners to visit six cemeteries and seven memorials. It is a trip we will always remember, seeing row upon row of pristine white stone, as if engraved yesterday, the serenity of the space in which our men were buried, and the splashes of colour from the flowers. It rained constantly which gave us a greater sense of connection to landscape and the past.

We were in awe, looking at the triumphant architecture of the memorials and overwhelmed by the vast collection of names. We photographed our men's graves and names, left a Titchfield poppy and wrote in the books of remembrance.

We have joined the vast numbers who will never forget.

Photographing Frank Stuart's name on the Vis en Artois Memorial

Titchfield Remembers Project

Finding Charlie Chalk at Queant Road Cemetery

Looking for Ernest Gamblin at Loos Memorial

Introduction

For many of the men who joined up in 1914 and those regulars who were already in the forces, going to war was a role their relatives and ancestors had performed before them.

Titchfield families had a hand in battles on land and water through many centuries, both as providers of skills and materials and as a rich source of fighting men willing or not.

Initially untrained Anglo Saxon villagers were obligated to take up arms and become a part-time army or 'Fyrd', in order to defend the area from invasion. Alfred the Great improved this inadequate system by training a specific group of local men to protect the Kingdom of Wessex and setting up the first organised navy to repel the Danes.

The ancient parish of Titchfield had a long stretch of coastline spanning about seven miles which made it ideal to head off attacks from the water. This south coast position also gave residents a ring side seat on skirmishes with Europe and with that, the possibility of economic growth. With the original tidal River Meon flowing past the village, many parishioners had a working relationship with the sea. There is evidence that in the 15th century the parish was a place to buy timber for ship building and skills for maintenance. In the 18th century Portsmouth dockyard used the local iron works at Funtley and as late as the 20th century Titchfield farmers had acquired the tender to supply cabbages to the Royal Navy.

During the 14th and 15th centuries home defence groups or 'Militias' were made up of young fit locals who were conscripted and trained to deal with the sporadic wars with France and beyond. The Muster Roll (the list of men) for The Titchfield Hundred of 1548 consists of fighting groups called Archers and Billmen (infantry with curved blades on poles). By the 1635 roll fighting terminology had changed to Musketeers, Pioneers and Corselettes (meaning light half armour) and both these rolls include familiar Titchfield names. Bowman, Burge, Emery, Longe, Monday and Smith can be read and are also on the Titchfield WWI Roll of Honour centuries later, though often the spelling has been modified.

By the mid 17th century the tradition of local part-time defence had waned, so when Charles II was restored to the throne he formed the very first Standing Army of full-time professionals. A third of servicemen whose lives are recalled in this book were 'regulars', so it is likely that during this time Titchfield men made the armed forces their profession and their life.

Naval 'impressment' into service was rife in Portsmouth during the 17th and 18th centuries. While no evidence has been found of Titchfield men being targeted, as villagers worked within the local merchant fleet, they may have been illegally caught by the 'press gang' while loading cargo in Portsmouth.

In the late 18th century the British Parliament requested a force of volunteer cavalry to be re-established. These men could be called upon to defend the country against the very real threat of invasion from France when the standing army was abroad. As the south coast would be the main target, the Hampshire Yeomanry (or Carabiniers) was formed and men from Titchfield joined up.

From the beginning to the end of the 19th century the army as a whole had grown to five times its size and there are records of permanent soldiers from Titchfield who served in the foot regiments. Henry Mabbott of the 41st Foot and George Ford of 35th Foot both fought in the War of 1812 against America.

William Henry Bevis, born in Titchfield, belonged to the impressive Naval Brigade and was awarded the Conspicuous Gallantry Medal in 1881 for his bravery in the first South African war. At the end of 1899 the regulations for the volunteer regiments changed to allow part-time servicemen to fight abroad. Able Seaman Arthur Couzens, Stokers Alfred and James Frampton and Gunner George Pharoah were among the local Carabiniers who took part in the 2nd Boer War and have their names on the village memorial. Private Moody died on 30th March 1902 also serving in South Africa with the 2nd Hampshires. As in so many cases he died in an unfortunate accident rather than at the hands of the enemy.

Titchfield village appears to have been a refuge for naval officers over the centuries and still is today. Illustrious residents included:

Edward Ives (1719-1786) - Naval surgeon

John Bourmaster (1735-1807) - Admiral of the Blue

Sir Richard King (1730-1806) - Rear Admiral of the White.

The village was also a source of well educated 'officer material'. A boy's preparatory school was based in the village throughout the 19th century where many men involved in the East India Company sent their sons to be schooled. In 1841 on the outskirts of the village Fosters Royal Naval Academy was established at Stubbington House. Thirteen WWI Royal Navy flag officers were schooled there and another alumni Captain Robert Falcon Scott, is famous for his epic journey in Antarctica.

When the lower ranks came home to the village after serving abroad, they often returned to local jobs as farmers or labourers. In 1881 there were about 15 retired naval servicemen residing in Titchfield, including James Gamblin and William West.

5th Nov 1912 Carnival 'Tableau' by the territorials L.C Lapsard, Pte Eyres, Fearne & C Bowers with Miss Matthews

On 19th November 1902 the village drill hall opened, providing the 'volunteers' with a permanent base. These regiments became the Territorial

Force in 1908, the precursor to what is now the Territorial Army. Caribineers (a later spelling) Wilfred Pharoah and James Tremlett began as volunteers and then later fought in the First World War.

Conscription was inevitable. In 1914 Britain had a professional army of 125,000 men. Germany had the immediate service of 840,000 men and Russia's standing army alone was 1.3 million.

Between 1914 and 1918 over 200 Titchfield men were called upon to fight. There were those who died during the four years from injury or illness and there were those who came home and had their lives shortened by the effects of war. And then there were the rest, whose lives were changed immeasurably.

This book is in recognition of the sacrifice of all Titchfield men.

The Memorial within St Peter's Church Titchfield

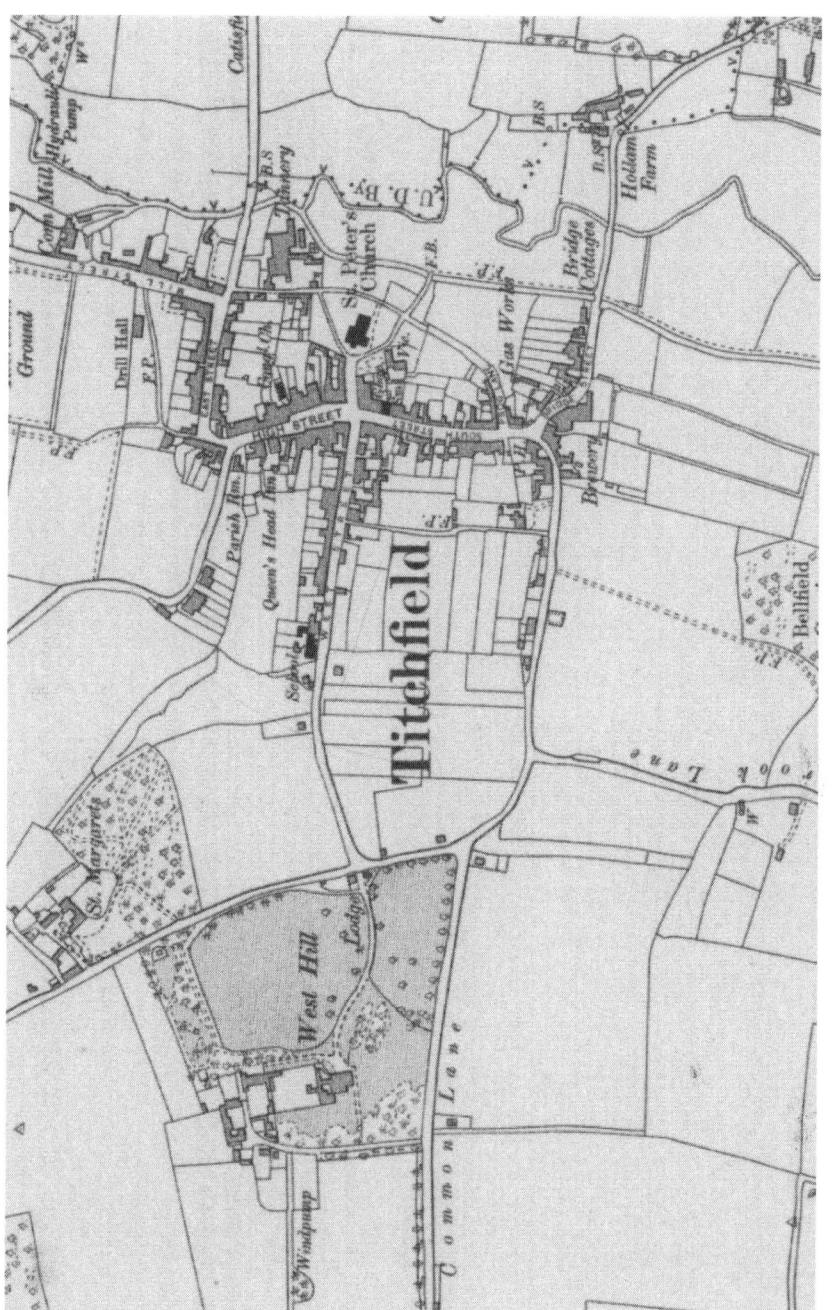

Titchfield street map of 1910

Those Who Gave Their Lives.

*William Arthur Barrow**
George William Bedford
Albert George Biddle and Frank Biddle
Frederick John (Fred) Bowers
Frederick John Bowers
Henry Walter Bowers
Ernest Charles Alfred Bowman
*Herbert Walter Bungey**
Francis Thomas Darrel Cade
Charlie Chalk
*John David Chase**
Harry Couzens
Henry John Edmunds
*James William Edmunds**
Arthur Sidney Fearne
John Henry Fleet
George Ford
*Frank Frampton**
Henry George Fry
Ernest Gamblin and Walter Robert Gamblin
William Henry Hatto
Ernest Henry Heath
Frederick Charles Leat
Ernest Frank Light
Reginald Thomas Marriott
*Charles Mathews**

William Thomas Matthews

Percy George Merritt

Arthur Newby and Frederick Newby

Ernest Edward Pharoah

Duncan Phelps

Arthur Price*

John Frank Price

Walter Reed*

William Sandy

John Sims

Albert Ernest Smith

Charles Smith*

Frank Sidney Smith*

Frank Smith and Walter Smith

Frank Stuart

Victor George Taylor

Donald Barfoot Edwards Upshall

Benjamin Waterfall*

Francis Edward Watts

Arthur Carnarvon Whittaker and
Carnarvon Lewis Whittaker

Thomas Henry Wright

* *Titchfield men added to the list in 2014*

William Arthur Barrow

Service:	1st London Regiment Royal Fusiliers 56th Battalion
Rank:	Private Service No. 204690
Birth:	1892 East St, Titchfield, Hampshire
Death:	25th Nov 1917 Louverval, Cambrai, France
Home Address:	Horsham, Sussex
Next of Kin:	Henry & Elizabeth Barrow

William Arthur Barrow was born at the Wheatsheaf public house on East Street. His father was a licensed victualler and he had two siblings Emily and Francis. The family moved on to run pubs in Bexley and Redhill, and by 1911 William had left home and was working as a servant in Horsham. He enlisted in Woolwich in 1914 and survived until The Battle of Cambrai in November 1917.

This campaign had strategic significance, as the area was the hub of German communications, serviced by road, rail and canal. Sir Douglas Haig described the objective for the Battle of Cambrai as the gaining of a *'local success by a sudden and unexpected attack'*. The proposed method of assault was new, with no preliminary artillery bombardment, just tanks to break through the German wire, with the infantry following under the cover of smoke shells. Allied aircraft flew around in the days before the attempt to capture Bourlon Wood, hoping that the noise would mask the assembly of more than 1000 guns and 476 tanks. It is clear from German reports that their intelligence had failed to predict what was to come.

On the 20th November, shrouded by mist and smoke, the British broke into apparently impregnable defences with few casualties. However, in the next five days much of the ground gained was retaken by the Germans. Attacks were beaten off and the heaviest casualties were incurred by the 1st/19th London Regiment who were so badly gassed that only 70 of them were still fit for duty by the end of the afternoon.

According to the 1st/19th Regimental War Diaries, B Company reported gas as "Not Tear Gas, a different kind". This was likely to have been mustard or chorine, the latter a yellow- green vapour that attacked the lungs and death when it occurred was akin to slow drowning.

On the evening of the 25th November a fresh attack by the enemy regained Bourlon Village. Our troops offered serious resistance and during this offensive it is likely that Private Barrow lost his life.

William is remembered here on the Cambrai Memorial, Louveral.

Titchfield Remembers Project

The Wheatsheaf public house, East St, circa 1900

William aged about three years old

GEORGE WILLIAM BEDFORD

Service:	1st East Yorkshire Regiment
Rank:	Private Service No. 30692
Birth:	1892 Titchfield
Death:	25th Apr 1918 Kemmelberg, Belgium
Home Address:	South Street Titchfield
Next of Kin:	Fanny Bedford, formally Singleton (nee Smith)

George grew up in Titchfield living in South Street and at eighteen he worked locally as a farm labourer, as was common for Titchfield lads. In 1914 he married a widow Fanny Singleton and adopted her three children. Their only child, George was born the following year. George senior enlisted with the 1st Battalion of the East Yorkshire Regiment in Gosport on 8th November 1915. He was wounded at Passchendaele in July 1917, but was back at the front nine months later.

Fortunate to have survived the First Battle for Kemmel Ridge, Private Bedford returned to the front line. During the night of the 23rd and 24th April he took part in the Second Battle, a ferocious fight to stop the German's getting behind Ypres and attacking from the south. The enemy bombardment consisted of shells (including gas), which reached not only the forward trenches, but also the communication trenches behind. With communication gone, the loss of their commanding officer and the enemy continuing to advance, the remaining 1st East Yorkshires retreated taking many wounded with them.

'In rushes from shell hole, to shell hole, turning occasionally to fire a few rounds at the enemy and then moving on again, these few survivors of a very gallant Battalion withdrew'

Before the 25th April the 1st Battalion of the East Yorkshire Regiment had reportedly consisted of around 500 men. By the end of the day it had 29. Four hundred and forty seven men were initially recorded as 'missing in action', one of those being George. His younger brother Sydney also enlisted and survived to live until 85 years old.

The Tyne Cot Memorial is one of four in Belgium commemorating the missing and bears the names of almost 35,000 men whose final resting places are unknown; among them is Private George Bedford. (c) CWGC

South Street Timber framed Cottages on right where Private Bedford lived, circa 1900

Private Bedford 1915

ALBERT GEORGE BIDDLE

Service:	2nd Battalion King's Royal Rifle Corps
Rank:	Rifleman Service No. 10363
Birth:	1894 Wickham, Hampshire
Death:	10th Jan 1915 Le Touret, France
Home Address:	Iron Mills Cottages, Titchfield
Next of Kin:	Harriett Jane Biddle (nee Smith)

Albert was one of ten children of Henry, a baker by trade living at Lavey Farmhouse near Funtley (Fontley) and his wife Harriett. On the 1911 census Harriett is shown as widowed and is living in nearby Iron Mills Cottages and Albert is described as a 'cowboy'. By November of that year Albert had enlisted as a regular soldier in the King's Royal Rifle Corps (KRRC) and his elder brother Frank into the Hampshire's.

The 1st Division were dispatched to France in August 1914. It included the 2nd Battalion KRRC who landed at Le Havre on the 13th August 1914. They fought on the Western Front throughout the war, taking part in most of the major actions including the 1st Battle of Ypres in October of that year.

The Defence of Givenchy took place between 23rd November 1914 and 6th February 1915 as part of the British Expeditionary Forces 'Winter Operations' on the western front

According to the 2nd Battalion KRRC Official War Diary troops were stationed south of Bethune, in trenches at Beuvry Wood. Conditions were poor, with shortages and bad weather. Rifleman Biddle was one of 31, whose body was not recovered.

On the 10th January a bombardment began across the canal towards the enemy and at 2pm an attack started, its aim to take a nearby observation post. Whilst initially successful, the attacking party lost 35 servicemen, many of them buried by the enemy trench collapsing and with only eight men left, they retreated.

Beyond the Memorial

Albert George Biddle is remembered on the Le Touret Memorial France.

Frank Biddle

Service:	10th Service Battalion Hampshire Regiment
Rank:	Private Service No. 10106
Birth:	1892 Titchfield, Hampshire
Death:	10th Aug 1915 Gallipoli, Turkey
Home Address:	Iron Mills Cottage, Titchfield
Next of Kin:	Harriet Jane Biddle (nee Smith)

Frank was the eldest son of Henry and Harriet and brother to Albert George (see previous page) and the family lived at Lavey Farm before moving to Iron Mills Cottages Fontley. Initially Frank worked on a local farm, but at the first call for troops he joined the Hampshire Regiment. The 10th Battalion moved to Dublin to train as part of the 10th (Irish) Division.

By July 1915 they had arrived off the coast of Lemnos, Greece as part of the 29th Brigade in preparation to land at Gallipoli. On the 7th August they arrived at Anzac Cove and took part in the Battle of Chunuk Bair, to take a mountain near the coast. The Turkish soldiers launched a fierce counter-attack, drove the British from their positions and then charged over the mountain towards the sea. Despite killing the Turks in large numbers using machine-gun fire and naval bombardment, the allied attack was deemed a failure.

The despatch of General Sir Ian Hamilton, Commander in Chief of the Mediterranean Expeditionary Force, printed in the Third Supplement to the London Gazette of 6th January 1916:

At daybreak on Tuesday, 10th August, the Turks delivered a grand attack from the line Chunuk Bair-Hill against these two battalions, already weakened in numbers, though not in spirit, by previous fighting....... The ponderous mass of the enemy swept over the crest, turned the right flank of our line below, swarmed round the Hampshire's and General Baldwin's column, which had to give ground, and were only extricated with great difficulty and very heavy losses.

Albert Ernest Smith, a neighbour at Iron Mills Cottages, also joined the 10th Hampshire Regiment and died on the 10th August 1915.

Privates Frank Biddle and Albert Smith are remembered on the Helles Memorial, Turkey, as are four other Titchfield men commemorated in this book.

Lavey Farm with cyclists Fred Couzens (brother to Harry in this book) his wife Elsie Down, her sister Amy and the new tenant of the farm Ruth Etherington. Circa 1930

Beyond the Memorial

The Soldier (1914)
Rupert Brooke

If I should die, think only this of me:
That there's some corner of a foreign field
That is forever England. There shall be
In that rich earth a richer dust concealed;
A dust whom England bore, shaped, made aware,
Gave, once, her flowers to love, her ways to roam,
A body of England's, breathing English air,
Washed by the rivers, blest by the suns of home.
And think, this heart, all evil shed away,
A pulse in the eternal mind, no less
Gives somewhere back the thoughts by England given;
Her sights and sounds; dreams happy as her day;
And laughter, learnt of friends; and gentleness,
In hearts at peace, under an English heaven.

Rupert Brooke died 23rd April 1915 before reaching Gallipoli

Frederick John (Fred) Bowers

Service:	14th Battalion Hampshire Regiment
Rank:	Private Service No. 12878
Birth:	1895 Titchfield, Hampshire
Death:	13th Oct 1916 Beaumont-Hamel, France
Home Address:	West Street, Titchfield
Next of Kin:	Alice Bowers (nee Godwin)

Fred was the sixth child and younger son of George Bowers, a bricklayer and Elizabeth Lock. Fred was 19 years old when he married Alice in the summer of 1915 and he enlisted in the 14th (1st Portsmouth) Battalion of the Hampshire Regiment. After training close to home, the battalion proceeded to France, landing at Le Havre on the 6th March 1916 and moving into northern France, as part of the 39th division.

There is a record in the Hampshire Regimental Journal that Fred was injured and evacuated to a casualty clearing station early in 1916, but he was back at the front within months.

The Battle of Ancre Heights was part of Hague's 'autumn offensive' to take Thiepval Ridge and its vital high ground. The 39th Division began their assault in the afternoon of the 9th October 1916. Between that day and the 14th October, when the operation to claim the Schwaben Redoubt was deemed successful, Private Bowers lost his life.

When a great-grand nephew visited Fred's grave he placed some Titchfield earth by his stone, *"a little piece of home for him"*.

Fred was buried at Hamel Military Cemetery, France within a few feet of Henry Edmunds another West Street lad

FREDERICK JOHN BOWERS

Service:	R.F.A. 19th Divisional Ammunition Column
Rank:	Lance Bombardier Service No 113602
Birth:	1898 Titchfield, Hampshire
Death:	5th May 1918 Calais, France
Home Address:	West Street, Titchfield
Next of Kin:	Fred & Martha Bowers (nee Smith)

Fred Bowers snr, a labouring tile maker had one son Frederick John and three daughters, Hilda, Lily and Florence.

Frederick enlisted in the Royal Field Artillery which was organised into small units or 'columns', to support divisions and was responsible for the medium calibre guns and howitzers deployed close to the front line. As part of the 19th Western Division, after training under canvas on Salisbury Plain, they proceeded to France in mid July 1915 and camped near the town of Saint Omer. This division was in action in most of the major battles of the Western Front, starting at The Battle of Loos that autumn, throughout the next two years and, for Frederick Bowers the final one, the last battles of the Somme in April 1918.

The division was in action for the early battles on the Somme, its great achievement being the capture of the village of La Boisselle. The cost to the 19th Division was around 3,500 and today their memorial stands in front of the village church. It was in this action that their first three VCs were awarded.

The division was again heavily involved in the German offensive in 1918 in several areas including the Aisne, where it had been sent for a rest. The Germans struck there just after the division had arrived. Between the start of the German offensive on the 21st March, and the end of May 1918 divisional casualties totalled 11,250.

During this attack the 19th Divisional Artillery fought with the greatest gallantry and fired their guns at point-blank range at the hostile infantry of the German Alpine Corps [A Short History of the 19th (Western) Division 1914-18 Pub.1919 J.F.C. Fuller]

Injured during the April offensive Lance Bombardier Bowers was evacuated to a clearing station and back to a field hospital near Calais. He died of his injuries on 5th May 1918, was buried in Les Baraques Military Cemetery and posthumously awarded the Croix de Guerre for his service to France.

The National School in West Street would have educated many of the boys in this book including Frederick and his older cousin Fred both of whom lived nearby.

Henry Walter Bowers

Service:	15th Battalion Hampshire Regiment
Rank:	Sergeant Service No. 19060
Birth:	15th Sept 1887 Fareham, Hampshire
Death:	23rd Mar 1918 Picardy, France
Home Address:	South Street, Titchfield
Next of Kin:	Thomas and Mary Bowers (nee Heath)

Thomas and Mary had two children Henry and Elsie. Thomas, from an old Titchfield family, was a cowman working at the Lunatic Asylum at Knowle, Fareham in 1881, and later a general labourer at the Tanneries in the village. As a young man Henry worked as a gardener, one of the local occupations, and a butcher's assistant. He was also a member of the part-time volunteer force, The Hampshire Yeomanry. He was still living at home with his parents in South Street when he joined the 15th Battalion Hampshire Regiment, one of Lord Kitcheners Pals Battalions on the 21st July 1915.

The 15th Hampshires Battalion arrived in France in May 1916, as part of the Fifth Army, 41st Division, 122nd Brigade and fought on the Somme, at Transloy Ridge and Kemmel. In November 1917 they travelled south through France, to shore up the Italian front. The same month the German High Command had started planning a decisive attack to take place the following spring, their target being the final destruction of the British Army before American Reinforcements could intercede. When this became known by the allies the 41st received orders in February 1918 to return to France.

The Battle of St. Quentin began on a misty day, 21st March 1918; the Germans fired one million artillery shells at the British Third and Fifth

Army, over 3,000 shells every minute. An attack by elite storm troopers followed and at the end of day one, 21,000 British soldiers were prisoners and the enemy had made great advances. The 22nd March was a day of intense fighting, the Fifth Army, under mounting pressure was unable to hold their part of the front and began retreating. Tragically, the Germans regained the Somme region from the Allies, where so many men, including Titchfield lads, had been killed in the battles of 1916.

Sergeant Bowers was killed in action and his body was lost in the retreat. He is commemorated on the Arras Memorial and mentioned in De Ruvigney's Roll of Honour (below) which says he is buried at Sapignies, north of Bapaume, though no grave has been identified.

His Commanding Officer wrote *"He was always a gallant and conscientious soldier. But a little longer and he would have had a commission, for which I strongly recommended him"*.

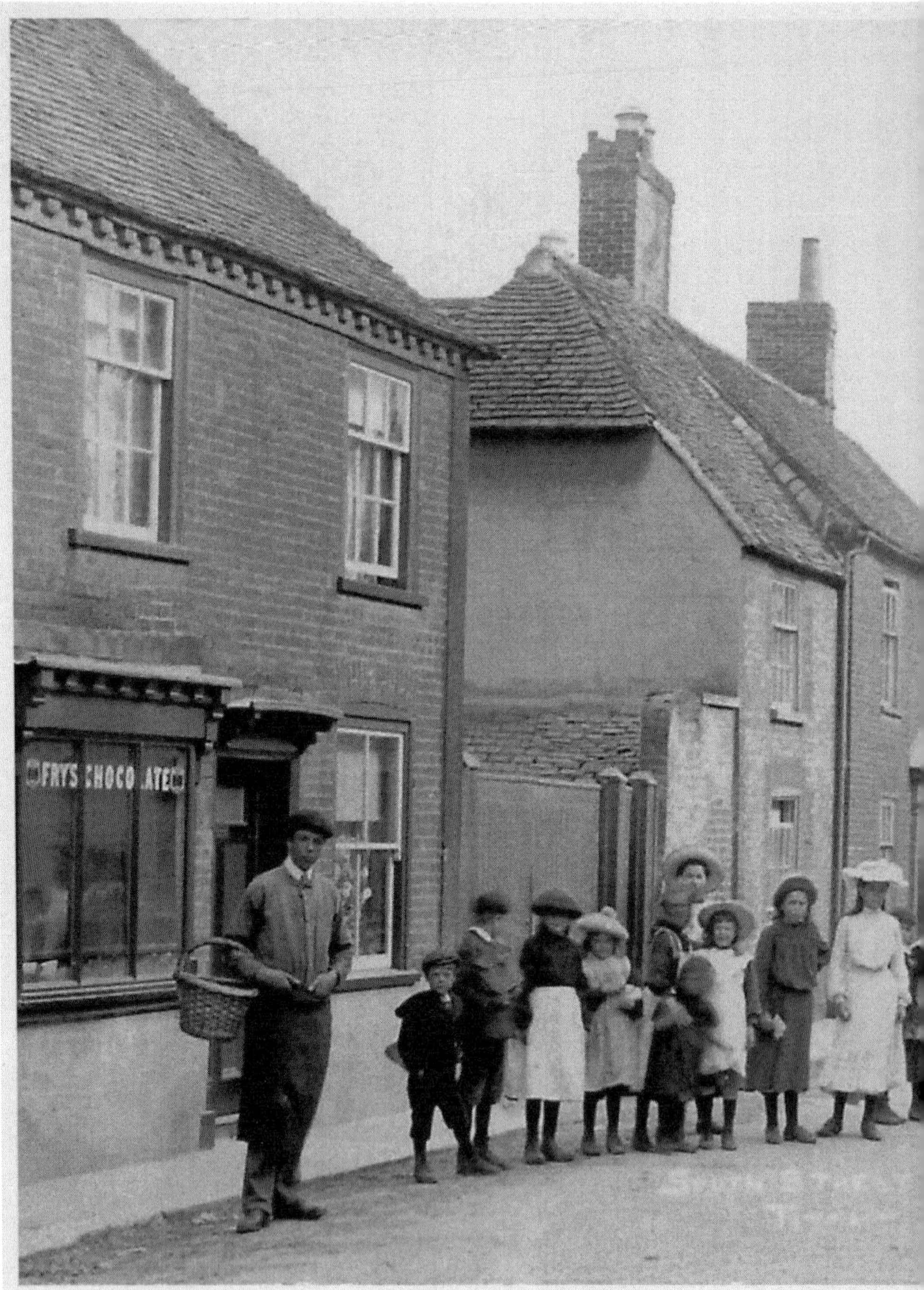
FRYS CHOCO ATE

The South Street Bowers family lived in one of the cottages at the far end on left (now demolished)

Ernest Charles Alfred Bowman

Service:	6th/2nd (Service) Battalion Wiltshire Regiment
Rank:	Private Service No. 27926
Birth:	1899 Hook in Warsash, Hampshire
Death:	2nd Nov 1918 Northern France
Home Address:	West Street, Titchfield
Next of Kin:	Charles and Jane Bowman (nee McEvely)

Ernest was the older child of Charles, a corn merchant and his wife Jane, a fruit picker in the local orchards. He joined up with the Hampshire Regiment in the spring of 1917, but saw active service with the Duke of Edinburgh's Wiltshire Regiment as part of the 19th Division. They were involved in the successful attack at Messines and saw heavy fighting on the Passchendaele Ridge. Due to heavy casualties, the 6th Battalion was disbanded in May 1918 and the remaining soldiers, including Private Bowman, were absorbed into the 2nd Battalion, 58th Brigade, 19th Western Division fighting with the Second Army.

Private Bowman fought at The Battle of The Selle, part of the Hundred Days Offensive, the final campaign of the western front. They were stationed at St Aubert and participated in successfully pushing the enemy back.

Sometime during this action Ernest was captured and interred in the Prisoner of War Camp at Hautmont. He died either of his wounds or disease and is buried at the Hautmont Communal Cemetery, northern France.

These West Street cottages, home to the Bowman family are still recognisable today

Herbert Walter Bungey

Service:	3rd Battalion Wiltshire Regiment
Rank:	Private Service No. 20172
Birth:	27th Mar 1895 Titchfield, Hampshire
Death:	17th Sep 1915 Weymouth, Dorset
Home Address:	West Street, Titchfield
Next of Kin:	William Bungey (brother)

In 1911 Herbert was a grocer's apprentice and was living in West Street, Titchfield with his widowed mother, Caroline, his older brother, William and his younger sister, Marjorie. He had grown up in Titchfield attending the local school until 1909. The family were well established in Titchfield and Herbert's mother Caroline ran a sweet shop in West Street.

Herbert enlisted with the Royal Field Artillery, but was later transferred to the Duke of Edinburgh's Wiltshire Regiment 3rd Battalion. During the war the 3rd Battalion was responsible for training recruits for overseas service, as well as carrying out home defence duties. Regimental records show that during 1915 the 3rd (Reserve) Battalion was stationed in Dorchester and then Weymouth.

Herbert died in 1915 aged just 20, he never married.

A newspaper report in the Western Gazette in September 1915 showed that an inquest held into his death showed that Private Bungey had become depressed. After his death, the Lance Corporal in charge noted that Herbert had been showing signs of depression and had been refusing food. He had only left the barracks once since his transfer there and although Herbert had not been in trouble before he failed to appear for guard duty the day before his death. He was arrested for this and reprimanded with a punishment of three extra guard duties, apparently a lenient sentence for war time.

We will never know the reasons for his depression, but he was a young man contemplating going to war. He had recently been transferred to the infantry, so was in unfamiliar circumstances and his mother, Caroline had passed away the year before. The verdict recorded was "Death by a gunshot wound, self-inflicted whilst in a state of unsound mind".

Private Herbert Bungey is buried in the Portland Royal Naval Cemetery, Dorset. (Image R.Boden)

WEST STREET, TITCHFIELD.

West Street after 1912 with the Bungey's house halfway up on the right and the new West End Inn on the left

Francis Thomas Darrel Cade

Service:	11th Battalion Hampshire Regiment
Rank:	Captain
Birth:	8th Oct 1894 Liverpool, Lancashire
Death:	6th Sep 1916 near Guillemont, France
Home Address:	The Surgery Coach Hill, Titchfield
Next of Kin:	Dr. Sidney and Ethel Cade (nee Exham)

Francis was the elder child of Titchfield village doctor Sidney and his wife Ethel. Sidney and Ethel, who were originally from County Cork had initially moved to Liverpool, where Francis was born. By 1898, when their daughter Lois arrived, the family was living in Sarisbury. Francis was educated at Edgborough, Guildford and was at Malvern College by April 1909. He became head of his house, a college prefect and a cadet officer in the O.T.C. In 1911, the family was living in the home on Coach Hill, Titchfield, now known as the old surgery.

Francis was proceeding to London University when the war broke out and he was given a commission in the Hampshire Regiment in September 1914. He was made a Lieutenant in July 1915, and was made Captain on 13th September 1916, one week after his death.

The 11th Battalion of the Hampshire Regiment was raised at Winchester in September 1914 as part of Kitchener's Second New Army and, after training they landed at Le Havre on the 18th December 1915 as part of the 16th Irish Division.

South of Delville Wood, the second German defensive system snaked down to the village of Guillemont. Enemy possession of Guillemont divided the allies' positions and prevented them from operating in unison. At noon on 3rd September 1916 the Fourth Army, including a brigade of the 16th (Irish) Division, advanced and after much fighting Guillemont was secured. Further advances beyond Guillemont were hampered by fierce German fire from nearby, so it was clear that capture of the wood and the village of Ginchy was essential. The 16th Division achieved these objectives three days later, but in the ensuing battle Lieutenant Cade was killed. His colonel wrote:

'He was one of my best young officers and I was very fond of him and I feel his loss deeply. He was a universal favourite with the officers and with his men.'

Prior to his death, Francis had received an official notification from the division General that he had distinguished himself by his gallant conduct and his devotion to duty in the field. He was posthumously promoted to Captain.

What Darrel Cade was as a soldier, he was every bit as much as a boy and a Prefect. Behind the gentleman, there was real strength. The high sense of duty, which he not only possessed but kept alive while at School, was not likely to fail him in a supreme hour. That it did not fail him, those who were with him when he fell, shot at close quarters, bear generous witness." Obituary in the November 1916 the Malvernian (College Magazine) and the Times Newspaper.

In December 1916 sister Lois started working at Hawkstone Hospital in Fareham, aged 18. As happened to so many women of her age she remained unmarried and lived until she was 85 years old.

Francis Cade at the beginning of the war

Captain Cade is remembered on the Thiepval Memorial in Northern France alongside 72,255 other servicemen from Britain and South Africa missing on the Somme

Charlie Chalk

Service:	26th Battalion Australian Infantry
Rank:	Private Service No. 4698
Birth:	1889 South Stoneham, nr. Southampton
Death:	3rd May 1917 Buissy, France
Home Address:	Mayburys, High Street, Titchfield
Next of Kin:	Daniel & Emily Jane Chalk (nee Couzens)

Daniel, a local fruit grower and his wife Emily had three children, the middle one was Charlie. After being educated locally at Blenheim House School, he left England to become a farmer, arriving first in Canada in 1911 and then on to Strathpine, an agricultural community in Queensland, Australia. His family homes were in Sarisbury, Hillhead and Fareham, but his parents were living at Mayburys, Titchfield by the time Charlie enlisted in the Australian Infantry in October 1915. After training he embarked from Sydney to join the war on Royal Mail Ship Mooltan on the 12th April 1916 arriving in France five months later as part of the 5th Infantry Brigade, 2nd Division.

The attack at Bullecourt on the 3rd May 1917 was a part of the Third Army offensive at Arras and was intended to be a diversionary attack to pin down German Reserves. It turned into two weeks of fierce fighting in which six British and Australian divisions took part under the enthusiastic but inexperienced Sir Hubert Gough. A previous attempt in April had been a disaster.

The night of the 2nd May was broken by bursts of shellfire by the Germans, using searchlights and firing mortar bombs towards the Allied front lines. Despite this activity the Australians assembled in their start positions without being detected and were ready to advance at 3.45 am.

They were ordered to advance at a steady walk with rifles at the trail, in order to have the energy to fight once faced with the enemy. The 15 pages of the war diary for the 3rd May details the events. An artillery bombardment on the German positions began in order to damage the German trenches and reduce defensive fire. However, the Germans had deep underground shelters, so that the damage was minimal and when the bombardment stopped, the Germans were ready for the advance. The Australians, moving at a steady walk, had scarcely reached the barbed wire when machine gun and rifle fire begun from the enemy causing many casualties. Snipers picked off the Australian officers and the advance became disorganised. Eventually the remaining Australian troops fell back to their own positions.

It has been commented that the Australians might have had more chance of success if they had charged the enemy lines.

For the gain of a kilometre around 7,000 Australians were killed at Bullecourt, 2,249 have no known grave.

Private Charlie Chalk's body was found, he is buried at Queant Road Cemetery. Buissy, France.

Mayburs around a decade before the Fielder Family rented the house to Mr & Mrs Chalk

John David Chase

Service:	27th Battalion Canadian Infantry
Rank:	Private Service No. 622389
Birth:	7th Nov 1887 Titchfield, Hampshire
Death:	4th Oct 1916 Contay, France
Home Address:	'Glenco', Bosham, Sussex
Next of Kin:	John and Elizabeth Chase (nee Chase)

Born in East Street Titchfield John David Chase and his twin Thomas Henry moved with their father, a farmer and mother to Beauworth near Arlesford, Hampshire and later to Bosham, Sussex. Both boys were educated privately in Chichester before Thomas became a teacher and John went travelling.

In April 1912 John sailed from Southampton to Portland, Oregan, USA and from there to Canada. Being a farmer's son, he may have been looking to establish a smallholding. In December 1914 he was back in England for a brief visit before returning to Canada in February 1915. He enlisted in the 27th Battalion (City of Winnipeg) of the Canadian Infantry on 1st April 1915 as part of the 2nd Contingent of the Canadian Expeditionary Force, arriving in France, via England in September of the same year.

As part of the 6th Infantry Brigade, 27th Battalion, 2nd Canadian Division, Private Chase arrived at the front just in time to take part in the heaviest fighting of the war, where it was said that the ranks fought with amazing tenacity.

At Ypres (St Eloi Craters and Mount Sorrel), the inexperience of their commanding officers cost many lives, but by the time they arrived at the Somme as part of the Fourth Army the Canadian tacticians had learnt quickly from earlier defeats.

At the Battle of Flers-Courcelette, with the addition of 'Land Ships' being brought into the battlefield for the first time, they confidently captured the Sugar and Candy trenches and the sugar refinery at Courcelette on 15th September. Although visually frightening to the enemy, the tanks proved very unreliable, but despite this the following day troops took Courcelette village. The 2nd Division achieved their objectives, but at a cost of 7,000 men. They went on to further success on 27th September at Thiepval Ridge and continued to prove a very effective fighting force for the rest of the war.

According to the 27th Battalion war diary 273 other rank servicemen were wounded between 25th and 29th September. Private Chase was among them. He was moved to the 49th Casualty Clearing Station at Contay suffering from gunshot wounds to his left thigh and right arm. He died from his wounds within days and is buried at the British Cemetery at Contay, France. His twin Thomas lived until he was 75.

Titchfield Remembers Project

In Flanders Fields (1915)
John McCrae

In Flanders fields the poppies blow
Between the crosses, row on row,
That mark our place; and in the sky
The larks, still bravely singing, fly
Scarce heard amid the guns below.
We are the Dead. Short days ago
We lived, felt dawn, saw sunset glow,
Loved and were loved, and now we lie
In Flanders fields.
Take up our quarrel with the foe:
To you from failing hands we throw
The torch; be yours to hold it high.
If ye break faith with us who die
We shall not sleep, though poppies grow
In Flanders fields.

The poet John McCrae died 28th January 1918, Boulogne Sur Mer

John Chase and his twin brother Thomas circa 1910

Harry Couzens

Service:	1st/7th Battalion Hampshire Regiment
Rank:	Private Service No.23042
Birth:	1890 Titchfield, Hampshire
Death:	16th Nov 1918 Yemen, (formerly Ottoman Empire)
Home Address:	Mill St, Titchfield
Next of Kin:	Gertrude May Couzens (nee Shawyer)

William a master baker and his wife Eliza King had seven children. Arthur, the eldest was in the Boer War and young Harry became an under gardener. Gertrude Shawyer worked as a servant in Fareham prior to her marriage to Harry in the autumn of 1915.

The 1st/7th Battalion of the Hampshire Regiment was a part-time battalion of the peacetime part-time Territorial Force, based in Bournemouth with the Hampshire Brigade, Wessex Division. Harry may have enlisted anytime after 1906, as the territorials took boys of 16. In August 1914 the Wessex Division was ordered to India to replace British and Indian regular army units who were to be deployed to the Western Front. They served in India until January 1918 when they were sent to Aden. The division, and the brigade, never saw action and were disbanded later in the war. The Hampshire Regimental Journal of December 1918 states that Private Couzens died of his wounds; the war diary for 16th November 1918 says he died from influenza.

During WWI influenza arrived in three waves. In spring 1918 there were some initial small outbreaks among the troops, with soldiers becoming ill with what was called three-day fever. Later that year it came back with a vengeance, infecting stressed-out and often malnourished soldiers. The onset was quick and fever could develop into bacterial pneumonia or bronchitis. Those who returned home at the end of their war brought with them the third wave of the illness into countries right across the globe.

Private Couzens died as a consequence of war during his defence of Aden.

(c) CWGPP

Henry John Edmunds

Service:	14th Battalion Hampshire Regiment
Rank:	Lance Corporal Service No.15013
Birth:	1891 Titchfield, Hampshire
Death:	3rd Sep 1916 Beaumont-Hamel, France
Home Address:	West Street, Titchfield
Next of Kin:	George and Elizabeth (nee Edmunds)

George, a farm labourer and Elizabeth had a family of nine children. Henry was a gardener at a gentleman's estate and in 1911 was still living at home in West Street with his widowed mother and two brothers. One of his older brothers, William also fought and died in WWI and is remembered in this book.

The 14th Battalion, Hampshire Regiment, also called 1st Portsmouth (Portsmouth Pals) was raised on the 3rd September 1914 as one of Lord Kitcheners 'Pals Battalions'. What is so impressive is that Portsmouth was able to amass enough men for two of these battalions (14th & 15th), when many in this town of enlistment age were already in the regular army or in the Navy. The 14th Hampshires joined the 39th Division arriving in France on the 6th March 1916.

Late on the 2nd September 1916 the division were preparing for an offensive, north of Hamel near the River Ancre on the Somme. This was the first British attack on the 1,000 mile German front at the village of Beaumont-Hamel since the disastrous failure on the opening day of the Somme on 1st July. On the 3rd September at 5.15am they moved off covered by machine gun fire, enabling the 39th Division to secure the German front line trenches against very little opposition. As they moved on to the final objective they came under heavy fire and were unable to get through the wire in front of the enemy positions. After fierce hand to hand fighting and their position had become untenable by 1pm, with casualties mounting and ammunition running short, they fell back. Sometime during that mornings action Lance Corporal Edmunds lost his life.

"The attack that day must have been a failure. The numbers of chaps killed or wounded was shocking to see. We did not even capture the German front line on our battle front.... afterwards there were only three of the old 5th Battalion left in my platoon" A Rough Diary of my Soldier Life, by Pte. George Linney 5th Battalion Royal Sussex Regiment

Henry is buried at Hamel Military Cemetery, France alongside just under 500 comrades.

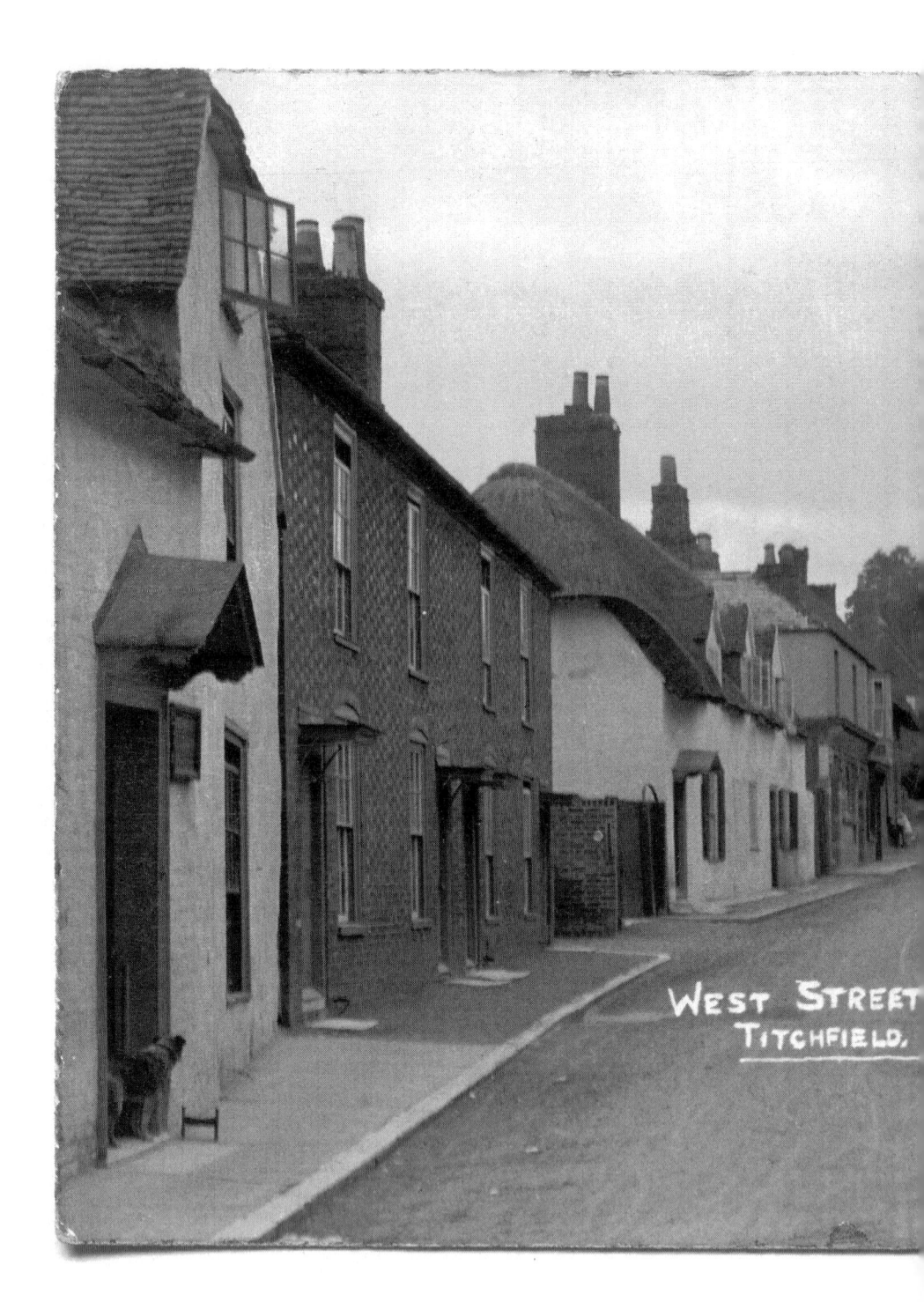

WEST STREET
TITCHFIELD.

West Street circa 1900 where the Edmunds family lived in one of the cottages on the right

JAMES WILLIAM EDMUNDS

Service:	13th Battalion Devonshire Regiment/Labour Corps
Rank:	Private Service No.145561/36043
Birth:	1880 Titchfield Common, Hampshire
Death:	31st Oct 1918 Oxford, Oxfordshire
Home Address:	Marine View, Titchfield Common
Next of Kin:	Elizabeth Edmunds (nee Whetren)

The Edmunds family were market gardeners living and working around the Strawberry fields of Titchfield. James, however, elected to train as a bricklayer. He married Elizabeth in 1902 and had two daughters, Elizabeth Violet and Lillian Rose. He enlisted in November 1915 at the age of 36, joining the Devonshire Regiment and later being transferred to the 28th Labour Corps. James was admitted to the 3rd Southern General Hospital Oxford, where he died of pneumonia. His medical records show that this was contracted while he was on active service at home.

The Labour Corps was formed in January 1917. Duties undertaken were road and railway building and repair, moving ammunition and stores and burial duties. In the UK they also carried out some work in agriculture, forestry and salvage. By the end of the war the Labour Corps accounted for around 400,000 men – more than 10% of the Army. Often recruits to the Corps were men who were not sufficiently fit for front line service or who had returned home wounded. Labour Corps units were sometimes deployed for work within range of the enemy, and this was particularly so in the spring of 1918 when they were used as emergency infantry on the Western Front.

The Corps was treated as a second class organisation. For example, men who died are commemorated under their original regiment, with the Labour Corps being secondary. Little is known about the day to day work of the Corps as few detailed records remain.

Private Edmunds was baptised James William and sometime in his 39 years his given names were reversed as can been seen here on his gravestone at St. Pauls Sarisbury Green.

Arthur Sidney Fearne

Service:	1st/4th Battalion Hampshire Regiment (TF)
Rank:	Sergeant Service No.280065 & 4/466
Birth:	1892 Titchfield, Hampshire
Death:	26th Jul 1916 Mesopotamia, (now Iraq)
Home Address:	The Hut, Common Lane, Titchfield
Next of Kin:	Albert and Mary Fearne (nee Daniels)

The second child and only son of Albert, a domestic gardener and Mary Fearne, Arthur became an under-gardener before he joined the 1st/4th Battalion sometime in 1915. By the time they arrived in Mesopotamia on the 25th October that year there had been an overly confident sense of superiority by the British and Indian forces over the Turks and during the move on Baghdad, senior tacticians encouraged by earlier successes had overstretched themselves. Sergeant Fearne, as part of the 35th Indian Brigade, cannot have been involved in much more than a steady retreat back to Kut, a town they captured earlier in the war followed by months of being trapped by the enemy.

The Ottoman Army surrounded Kut and the British-Indian fighting force were left to starve or die from malaria, cholera or injury for five months. Despite attempts to re-capture Kut and to barter their way out with offers of gold to free the besieged garrison, General Townsend eventually had to surrender on morning of 29th April 1916, after 147 days. For the British and Indian troops who had survived the siege, worse things were to come. On 6th May, the Turks began the 1,200-mile forced march of the prisoners across the Syrian Desert from Kut. Starvation, thirst, disease, and exhaustion reduced the number still further. Once at Baghdad the Turks paraded the prisoners through the streets and the defeat at Kut marked an important step towards the collapse of the British Empire. In November 1918, the official British report declared that 3,290 British and Indian POWs from Kut-el-Amara had died in Turkish captivity, while an additional 2,222 were missing and presumed dead. In all 20,000 men were lost in the attempts to retake Kut.

"For about a week they started to march us on to Baghdad..... We were very weak at the time, and just [had] to march along as best as we could. But all the time they were behind you, hammering you, hitting you on the back with a rifle...... When we got to Bagdad there was a mob of Arabs there, throwing mud and spitting on us" Private R Hockaday of the Queen's Own Royal West Kent Regiment also took part in the retreat to Kut and survived.

Hampshire Regiment records state that Sergeant Fearne died a prisoner of war, and his death may have happened at a railway terminus. Clearly he made it to Baghdad or close by, and was brought into the town for burial in the War Cemetery. A memorial in St Paul's Cathedral, London reads:

Kut-el-Amara
5 December 1915 to 29 April 1916
To the memory of
5746 of the garrison who died in the siege
or afterwards in captivity.
Erected by their surviving comrades

John Henry Fleet

Service:	14th Battalion Hampshire Regiment
Rank:	Lance Corporal Service No.15104
Birth:	1880 Titchfield, Hampshire
Death:	28th Oct 1916 Boulogne, France
Home Address:	South Street, Titchfield
Next of Kin:	Alice Fleet (nee Pack)

John Henry was the oldest child of John, the local miller and his wife Mary Shawyer and was brought up first in Mill Street, then South Street. He married Alice in the autumn of 1902 and settled in Fareham where John was a labourer. They had six children Reginald, Frederick, William, Alfred, Edith and Rosetta. Sometime in September 1914 John enlisted in the 14th Battalion Hampshire Regiment (Portsmouth Pals) and after training left for France, arriving on the 6th March 1916 as part of the 39th Division.

The Battle of Ancre Heights was part of Haig's large-scale autumn offensive to secure the whole of the Thiepval Ridge, and thereby have observation over the Upper Ancre, the vital high ground. After early successes the weather and appalling battlefield conditions delayed further operations; it was not until 21st October that renewed efforts against the Regina and Stuff trenches were possible. The attack was made up of the 14th Hampshires on the left, the 11th Royal Sussex in the middle and the 13th Royal Sussex on the right, advancing in three waves. The whole of the crest of the ridge was now in British hands, but casualties were high. A vivid description of the conditions in Stuff Trench was provided by Edmund Blunden (11th Royal Sussex) in his memoir, *'Undertones of War'*.

John is recorded in the Regimental Journal as having 'died of wounds'. He is buried in the Wimereux Communal Cemetery near Boulogne. His younger brother Sidney Charles of the Hants 1st Battalion died four days before John, and is remembered on the Thiepval Memorial. His brothers George and William survived the war, but his nephew William Mathews was killed two months before him and is remembered in this book.

John Fleet grew up in one of the cottages on Mill Street at the far end where the bypass now runs

GEORGE FORD

Service: Royal Navy HMS Good Hope

Rank: Petty Officer 1st Class   Service No.285093

Birth: 23rd Aug 1879 South Street Titchfield

Death: 1st Nov 1914, west of Isla Santa Maria

Home Address: West St. & South Street, Titchfield

Next of Kin: Charlotte Ford (nee Avery)

Petty Officer George Ford was the sixth of seven children born to James, an agricultural labourer from London and Hannah May White from Shedfield. They were living in West Street in 1871 and moved to The Red House yard in South Street for the next 30 years.

George joined the Navy on the 20th April 1897; his enlistment papers describe him as 5 feet 5 inches tall with brown hair and blue eyes. In between appointments at sea he found time to court and marry Charlotte Avery in 1905. At the outbreak of war he was on HMS Good Hope which was sent to reinforce Rear-Admiral Sir Christopher Cradock's British South America Squadron, becoming his flagship at the Battle of Coronel on the 1st November 1914.

Cradock set sail north from the Falklands to meet the enemy off the coast of Chile. The two opposing squadrons met at 5pm 50 miles west of Coronel. The British Squadron was made up of two obsolete armoured cruisers 'Good Hope' and 'Monmouth' (newly-commissioned with large numbers of reservists), an armed merchant cruiser 'Otranto' and the modern light cruiser 'Glasgow'. The Germans had two modern armoured cruisers and three light cruisers. Vice Admiral Graf Von Spee held all the aces: speed, longer range guns and better trained crews, so Cradock tried to force the action while the setting sun was behind him, blinding the enemy. But instead von Spee waited until around 7pm for the sun to set, leaving the British ships silhouetted and his own ships lost in the dusk before opening fire. After three hours fighting HMS Good Hope was blown up and HMS Monmouth sunk with a total loss of 1,570 men. Glasgow and Otranto disengaged and escaped to the south.

LOGS FOR NOVEMBER 1914 HMS GLASGOW
1 November 1914   at sea   Lat -36.9, S Long -73.63W
7.02pm: Enemy opened fire
7.06pm: Opened fire at 3rd ship in enemy's line
7.40pm: 'Good Hope' drew out of line
7.50pm: 'Good Hope', who was badly on fire, blew up
8.10pm: Ceased firing. Proceeded full speed out of action with "Monmouth" to westward
8.50pm: Lost sight of 'Monmouth' to NE
9.25pm: Observed enemy using searchlight & firing, presumably at "Monmouth"

Petty Officer Ford is commemorated at St. Peter's church Titchfield and on the Portsmouth Naval Memorial panel 3.

Frank Frampton

Service:	15th Reserve Battery Royal Field Artillery
Rank:	Driver Service No.58283
Birth:	1888 Titchfield, Hampshire
Death:	28th Mar 1915 Milton Hospital, Portsmouth
Home Address:	Lea Mount, Titchfield Common
Next of Kin:	William & Louisa Frampton (nee Whitear)

Frank was one of seven children from an old Titchfield family of agricultural labourers, and was brought up in Posbrook Lane and Hunts Pond Road, outside the village. Frank was a farm worker before enlisting in the Royal Field Artillery.

On entering the Artillery as a Gunner, Frank would have used his farm skills in working with horses to be promoted to 'Driver'. His role was to 'drive' the gun into position with horses and he was also trained to drive a horse drawn vehicle, including gun teams and ammunition wagons. When the guns were in action, he would have remained at the wagon lines and assisted in the supply of ammunition. His uniform reflected the RFA heritage, as they were still dressed in breeches and long boots like mounted soldiers.

It appears that the 15th Reserve Battery stayed at Larkhill Training Camp for the duration of the war. The role of the Reserve Batteries, besides being in the front line, was as a mobile artillery force in the event of an invasion, static defence in key places such as ports and to train new recruits in the skills of artillery warfare.

Driver Frampton became ill with scarlet fever and was transferred to the Milton Fever Hospital in Portsmouth. Before the availability of antibiotics, a number of infectious diseases, including measles and scarlet fever were life threatening. The latter sometimes could develop complications such as rheumatic fever and multiple organ failure. Servicemen dying from illness accounted for one third of the total lost in WWI.

Driver Frank Frampton died from the complications of scarlet fever and is buried in Milton Cemetery, Portsmouth.

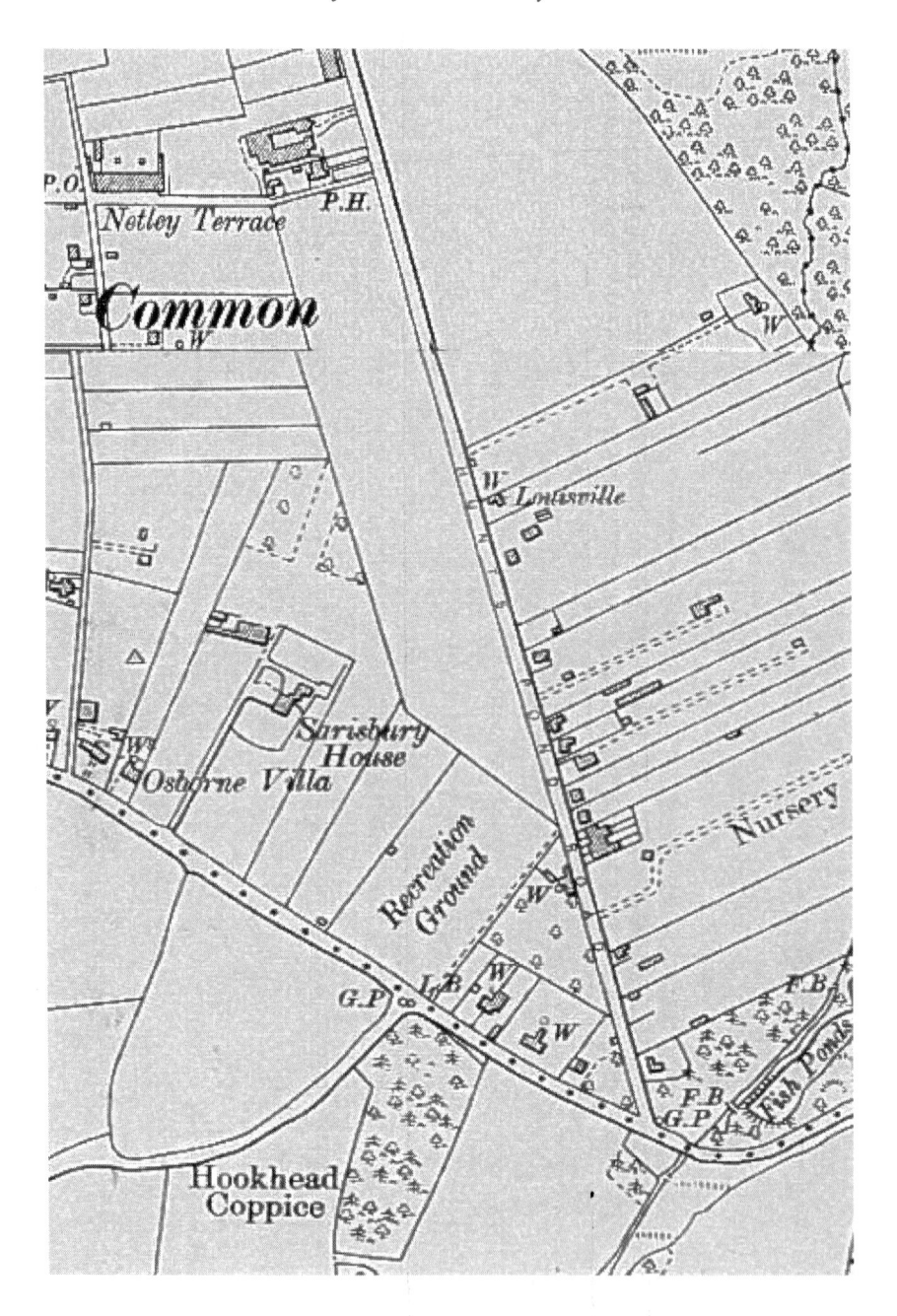

Frank Frampton grew up in Hunts Pond Road just outside Titchfield, surrounded by strawberry fields

Frank Frampton in full RFA uniform

(Henry) George Fry

Service:	5th Brigade Royal Field Artillery
Rank:	Lance Bombardier (driver) Service No.76595
Birth:	1896 Titchfield, Hampshire
Death:	14th Jun 1918 Pernes, France
Home Address:	West Street, Titchfield
Next of Kin:	Andrew & Alice Fry (nee Frost)

George as he was known, was the eldest son of Andrew, a Titchfield bricklayer and his wife Alice, whose previous husband William Pack, a West street lad, had died leaving her with three young children. George was brought up with his half siblings and enlisted at Gosport with his half brother Frederick, who survived the war.

A 'Driver' in the context of the RFA at this time required extra training to manoeuvre the guns into position using the horses, so he wouldn't have arrived in France until 1915.

Lance Bombadier Fry was initially part of the Fifth Army, but just before the offensive in the Champagne region of France at the end of May 1918, it was renamed the Fourth under a new General. During this period in the war, the Germans launched a massive and sustained gas attack. There is documentary evidence that a number of RFA servicemen were affected by gas and transported to the 6th, 22nd and 13th clearing stations at Pernes, where they died.

It is very likely that Lance Bombardier Fry also died from gas poisoning.

His younger brother Sidney joined the 1st Dorset Regiment briefly but was dismissed in May 1917, for being under age or unfit for duty. Sidney died in 1923 along with his daughter Violet.

Georges' half sister Alice Beatrice Pack married John Henry Fleet, who was killed in France and is also remembered in this book.

Henry George is buried in the Pernes British Cemetery alongside 1,077 other servicemen

Ernest Frank Gamblin

Service:	6th Hampshire & 2/6th Royal Warwickshire Regiment
Rank:	Private Service No.1656 & 6226
Birth:	1897 Titchfield, Hampshire
Death:	19th Jul 1916 Fromelles, France
Home Address:	St. Margarets Farm, Titchfield
Next of Kin:	George and Margaret Gamblin (nee Emery)

George, an Agricultural Labourer and his wife Margaret had nine children. Ernest, his six brothers and two sisters were brought up at St. Margaret's Farm, Titchfield before moving to Cranleigh in Surrey. Ernest originally joined the 6th Hampshire Regiment, but later was attached to the 2nd/6th Battalion of the Royal Warwickshire Regiment, 182nd Brigade, part of the 61st (2nd South Midland) Division. They spent the first year on home guard, before arriving in France in May 1915. The battalion had seen little front line experience other than a few trench raids before 19th July 1916.

The Battle of Fromelles was a two day conflict fought in northern France by 61st British Division and 5th Division of the Australian Imperial Force (AIF.) Its aim was to keep German forces from being redeployed at the Battle of the Somme, which had been raging for over two weeks. Initially only an artillery barrage was planned, as a way of fooling the enemy into thinking a full scale assault was imminent. However, despite having primarily inexperienced divisions at his disposal, Commander in Chief Douglas Haig requested offensive plans to be drawn up to take new ground along a two mile stretch of the German front line. The battle was a complete failure with heavy troop losses and no ground gained. Seven hours of shelling had little or no effect on the

German strong points (as scouting parties reported at the time) and bright summer daylight made advancing troops easy targets. Poor communication, continuous plan changes and the strength of the enemy was underestimated, all of which led to over 7,000 killed, wounded or missing from the two divisions.

The Gamblin family lost five of their sons as a result of the war. Ernest and Walter are remembered in this book. Henry and John died in March 1919 from influenza and William in 1925.

In 2009 the bodies of around 300 British and Australian soldiers from the Battle of Fromelles were exhumed from a mass grave which had lain undisturbed for 93 years. They were re-interred in a new cemetery at Pheasant Wood with full military honours. Through DNA tests some servicemen were identified but others are yet to be given their name; Private Ernest Gamblin was sadly not found among them.

The missing included Private Gamblin, who is remembered on the Loos Memorial.

No Man's Land (1976)
Eric Bogle

Well, how'd you do, Private Willie McBride,
D'you mind if I sit down here by your graveside?
I'll rest for awhile in the warm summer sun,
Been walking all day, Lord, and I'm nearly done.
I see by your gravestone you were only nineteen
When you joined the glorious fallen in 1916,
I hope you died quick and I hope you died "clean,"
Or, Willie McBride, was it slow and obscene?
"The sun how it shines on the green fields of France
The warm wind blows gently, and the red poppies dance
And look how the sun shines from under the clouds
There's no gas, no barbed wire, there's no guns firing now
But here in this grave yard that's still No Man's Land
The countless white crosses in mute witness stand
To man's blind indifference to his fellow man
And a whole generation who were butchered and damned."

Beyond the Memorial

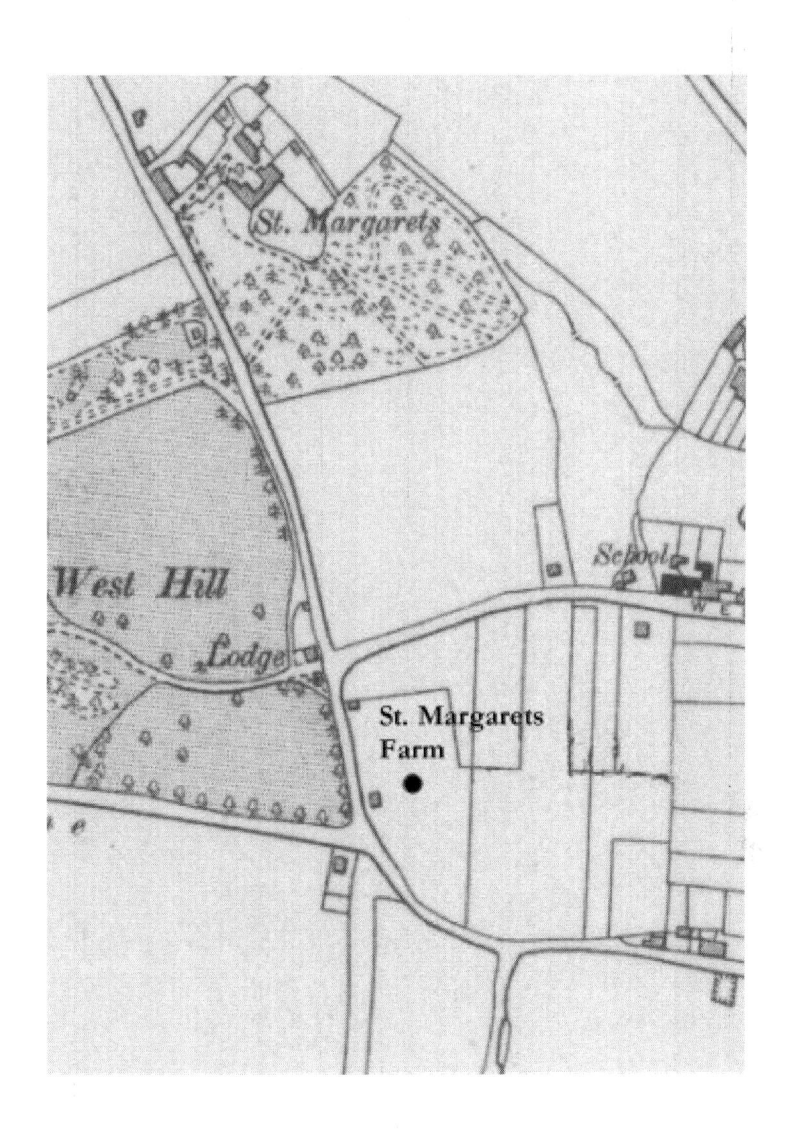

Location of the family small holding at the top of the village

Walter Robert George Gamblin

Service: 1st Portsmouth Battalion (Drake) RMLI

Rank: Lance Corporal Service No. PO/15352

Birth: 22nd Sep 1888, Warsash, Hampshire

Death: Apr/May 1915 Gallipoli, Turkey

Home Address: St. Margaret's Farm, Titchfield

Next of Kin: George and Margaret Gamblin (nee Emery)

Walter was the oldest of nine children. His father, George was an agricultural labourer and the family lived at St. Margaret's Farm before moving to Cranleigh in Surrey. Walter enlisted on the 30th September 1908 in the Royal Marine Light Infantry (RMLI) which, at that time, put prospective long service recruits through a rigorous enlistment training process. The RMLI were trained as naval gunners as well as infantry soldiers, so once on board the marines would be responsible for at least one main gun turret. In 1923 the RMLI was renamed The Royal Marines.

The Portsmouth Battalion boarded the ship 'Gloucester Castle' in Bristol on 27th February 1915, before setting sail the following day for East Africa. Soon the marines learnt their destination had changed; they were now to join a truly multi- national task force at Gallipoli with the aim to clear a path through the Dardanelles strait to allow allied shipping to pass through and support Russia.

The Gallipoli Campaign began on the 28th April with the RMLI moored off Skyros in a storm, waiting for the weather to improve. On 29th they disembarked and got into position alongside the Australian & New Zealand Army Corps (Anzac); all they saw were deep gullies ahead of them and hills overhead. There was minimal cover and there were many killed building trenches during the next two days. On the 1st May the Turkish attack began, repelled by the 1st Portsmouths, but the juxtaposed forces fared badly leaving the marines exposed. They hung on "by the skin of their teeth" lying in shallow trenches at the crest of the hills. Naval bombardment supported troops at dusk on 2nd May, which initially subdued the enemy and allowed the Marines and Anzacs to move to a ridge called Monash Valley towards Razer Back Hill. Soon fighting resumed in intensity and on 3rd May the Portsmouth Battalion was ordered to launch a counter attack along what became known as Dead Man's Ridge. The remnants of the Portsmouth Battalion gained a small foothold on the ridge top, but were left stranded without ammunition and other supplies. This attempt to retrieve a battle already lost resulted in the unnecessary slaughter of many more brave officers and men. A truce to bury the dead on both sides was not achieved until after 11th May.

L/Cpl. Gamblin was killed in action sometime between 28th April and 3rd May 1915 and is commemorated on the Helles Memorial, Gallipoli. He was the first of six Titchfield men out of about 5,000 allied troops to be killed before evacuation began in early November.

The RMLI passing through Titchfield Square 1915

Helles Memorial Gallipoli, Turkey

WILLIAM HENRY HATTO

Service:	1st Battalion Hampshire Regiment
Rank:	Sergeant Service No.7236
Birth:	1886 Portsmouth, Hampshire
Death:	3rd Nov 1914 Bailleul, France
Home Address:	Santa Rosa, Bridge Street, Titchfield
Next of Kin:	Mary Hatto (nee Hyslop)

William Henry was the oldest son of William, a labourer at a timber yard and Amelia Cook, who brought up their family of thirteen in Portsmouth. William jnr. joined the Army on 2nd August 1904, having been a painter's labourer and was stationed at Aldershot with the 1st Battalion, Hampshire Regiment. In the autumn of 1911, he married Mary Hyslop, a Portsmouth tailoress. Their son, Leslie William was born on the 11th November 1913 and by the following year they had moved to Titchfield.

The German and Allied Armies first came face to face at the First Battle of Ypres in mid October 1914. Battles took place for Messines south of Ypres involving the 1st Hampshires as part of the 4th Division. The French and British forces held onto Ypres and denied the German commanders a route across Belgium to the French coastal ports of Calais and Dunkirk, where they might have stopped the British troops from disembarking. In late October 1914, the 4th Division defended the sector of Ploegstreet Wood to St. Yves. Sometime during these days Sergeant Hatto was injured and was evacuated to the nearby hospital at Bailleul (2nd Casualty Clearing Station). On the 3rd November heavy enemy shelling badly damaged the hospital, as the monument in the town square attests. It is believed that Sergeant William Henry Hatto died during that shelling alongside two other patients.

Beyond the Memorial

Bailleul Communal Cemetery, France where William is buried together with Privates J Mitchell and T Hay. (Image Margaret Quinell)

Ernest Henry Heath

Service:	Army Veterinary Corps (att. 14th Indian Division)
Rank:	Sergeant Service No.SE 4075
Birth:	1884 Titchfield, Hampshire
Death:	21st Dec 1917 Baghdad, Mesopotamia
Home Address:	East Street, Titchfield
Next of Kin:	Florence Amelia Heath (nee Bartlett)

Ernest was baptised in Titchfield on 4th May 1884 into the long established Heath and Frampton families, his father Henry was a bricklayer and his grandfather a carpenter. By the age of seventeen, Ernest was apprenticed to a butcher and joined the Dragoon Guards Reserve a year later. In 1911 he married Florence Amelia Bartlett, a family friend from Portsmouth and the following year their son Henry Ernest was born.

Ernest was discharged from the Army Reserve after twelve years served and within months he rejoined at the outbreak of hostilities. By January 1915, Private Heath was serving in France with the Army Veterinary Corps (AVC). The following year he was transferred to the Mesopotamia Expeditionary Force, where he became Acting Sergeant.

At the outbreak of war, eleven Mobile Veterinary Sections plus six Veterinary Hospitals joined the first wave of troops. The mobile sections were equine versions of casualty clearing stations, evacuating horses suffering from battle injuries, exhaustion, mange and gas attacks. The Army Veterinary Corps increased its size four times to cater for the influx of horses being used for the cavalry, transport and artillery, both engaged on the Western Front and within the Ottoman Empire, where they also worked with camels. They treated over 2.5 million veterinary cases during the war, with impressively detailed records of each horse in their care; it shows, as over three quarters were found fit to return to duty. In addition to horses, other animals treated included message sending dogs and pigeons and canaries used to signal the presence of gas. There was an informal use of cats to keep down the rat infestation in the trenches, *"They were hungry and as big as cats,"* (Harry Patch 1898-2009) and as morale boosting pets such as Togo the cat on HMS Dreadnought.

British reinforcements in Mesopotamia in May 1917 were absorbed into the 14th Indian Division, supported by their No. 1 Mobile Veterinary Section. The 36th Brigade of the 14th Indian Division formed the Garrison of Baghdad.

The summer of 1917 was one of the hottest on record, so as fighting subsided, the enemy for a few months became the sun, the dust, and the flies. This must have been intolerable for the soldiers in tents and dugouts still clad in the winter uniforms. War correspondent Edmund Candler recalled *"The flies were unbelievable. You could not eat without swallowing flies. You waved your spoon in the air to shake them off: you put your biscuits and bully beef in your pocket and surreptitiously conveyed them in closed fist to your mouth, but you swallowed flies all the same"* These conditions led to appalling levels of sickness and death through disease. Cholera, smallpox, and dysentery were common and one of these caused the death of Acting Sergeant Heath. Ernest was buried at the North Gate War Cemetery, Baghdad, now Iraq.

Frederick Charles Leat

Service:	Royal Navy HMS Queen Mary
Rank:	Petty Officer Stoker Service No. 361751
Birth:	7th Apr 1887 Fareham, Hampshire
Death:	31st May 1916 Battle of Jutland, North Sea
Home Address:	High Street, Titchfield
Next of Kin:	Florence Eva Leat (nee Jeans)

Frederick was the fifth of seven children to William Leat and Emma Judd. William was a coachman from Southampton and by 1901 Emma was a widow living in Titchfield with her three daughters and Frederick, a Telegraph Messenger boy.

On the 22nd September 1903 Frederick joined the Royal Navy, but as normal in peacetime was often on leave. He married Florence Eva Jeans in 1909 and had three sons; Frederick born in 1910, Alfred in 1912 and Arthur in 1915.

The Battle of Jutland is considered to be the only major naval battle during the war and was fought by the British Grand Fleet on the 31st May and 1st June 1916 against the German High Seas Fleet in the North Sea, off the Jutland Bank to the west of Denmark.

At the beginning of the war the British had the superior fighting power at sea and so the Germans were intent on avoiding the main British Fleet. Due to the interception and decoding of German plans to target the British coastline, the whole British Fleet set sail to engage the enemy. Both fleets sailed in a similar formation, with a scouting squadron of battle cruisers sailing ahead of the main fleets. The British forward scouting party of six ships spotted five German battle cruisers and firing commenced. The enemy returned south to rendezvous with the main German fleet, which were a short distance away. The British squadron gave chase and when the main German fleet was sighted, they turned north to draw the enemy towards the British Grand Fleet which was heading towards the battle. Positioned in a semi circle ahead the entire British Fleet opened fire on the unsuspecting enemy who ran for home. The faster British ships gave chase and when they caught up with the Germans Queen Mary was targeted by two of the German ships and three enemy shells struck her. At first she did not appear to be severely damaged, but shortly after, the ammunition magazines exploded tearing the ship apart and sinking her in minutes. From the initial explosions, the debris from further blasts, the suction caused by the ship sinking and being trapped in the engine rooms, 1,267 men lost their lives. 21 survived by being picked up by British and German ships.

Although more British ships were sunk, the Germans had greater overall damage to their fleet which effectively ended any threat from above the water and so for the rest of the war the enemy concentrated on wreaking havoc from below using U-boats.

PO Leat is commemorated on four memorials: St. Peter's Church Titchfield, St. Luke's Church Portsmouth, Portsmouth City War Memorial and panel 16 of the Portsmouth Naval Memorial.

The wreck of HMS Queen Mary was found in 1991 and is protected by law.

The Leat family lived in the cottage on the far left of the High Street

Frederick Leat early on in his naval career

Ernest Frank Light

Service:	15th Battalion Hampshire Regiment
Rank:	Private Service No.20613
Birth:	1895 Titchfield, Hampshire
Death:	23rd Nov 1916 Voormezeele, Belgium
Home: Address:	West Street, Titchfield
Next of Kin:	Thomas & Selina Light (nee Shawyer)

Ernest was the fifth child and youngest son of Thomas and Selina Light. Thomas worked as an agricultural labourer, but sadly by 1911 he had been admitted to the Hants County Lunatic Asylum in Knowle, Fareham.

Ernest, a farm labourer joined the 15th Battalion Hampshire Regiment (2nd Portsmouth), one of the Pals Battalions in April 1915. They joined the 122nd Brigade, 41st Division to train at Aldershot. After 6 months they moved to France in early May, where they saw action, as part of the Fourth Army in various battles of the Somme. Private Light survived the infamous first day, the battle of Albert, where the 4th Army suffered nearly 58,000 casualties and the Battle of Flers-Courcelette where tanks were used for the first time. Private Light was also engaged in the Battle of the Transloy Ridges in October, which was the last time they saw direct action before the terrible weather that finally halted the offensive in November. According to the 15th Hampshire Official War Diary light duties were performed for a while. On the 20th November, medals were presented to the men who had fought at the battles of the Somme and then on the 23rd they moved up the line to relieve another brigade. On this day Private Light died, possibly of illness as there is no mention of casualties throughout November. Ernest's brothers Arthur and John survived the war.

Ernest is buried at Voormezeele Enclosures Cemetery in Belgium.

WEST ST, TITCHFI

Ernest and his family lived in one of the old cottages at the top of West Street.

Reginald Thomas Marriott

Service:	Royal Engineers Postal Section
Rank:	Corporal Service No.27502
Birth:	1891 Christchurch, Dorset
Death:	20th Feb 1919 Belgium
Home Address:	The Cottage, High Street, Titchfield
Next of Kin:	Thomas & Clara Marriott (nee Barton)

Reginald was the only child of Thomas and Clara Marriott, brought up in the bakery and confectioners in the High Street. His chosen profession was the postal service, working in Fareham by 1908, then briefly at Bridport Sorting Office in 1911 and back in Fareham the following year.

The Royal Engineers Postal Section served throughout the First World War on all fronts. In addition to mail delivery, the GPO also set up telecommunications between headquarters and the front line. On its journey to the Western Front, the post was delivered by army lorry to Folkestone or Southampton, where ships took at the height of the war, on average 12 million letters each day across to APS depots in Calais, Le Havre and Boulogne. Trains ran under cover of darkness dropping off mail along the route, taking only two days to reach the Western Front. Regimental orderlies would sort post and deliver to individual soldiers on the front line, and the objective was to hand out letters from home with the evening meal. Letters back to England were collected from field post offices which were as well equipped as sub post offices back home. The effect that 'morale boosting' letters from home had on servicemen cannot be underestimated and postal workers were a tremendous asset to the war effort.

Corporal Marriott survived the war, but sadly succumbed to pneumonia while still on active service. His will included a beneficiary called Natalie May Sandy, a milliner from Fareham; perhaps she was Reginald's intended.

Reginald is buried in the Halle Communal Cemetery, Belgium.

Charles Matthews

Service:	2nd Battalion Hampshire Regiment
Rank:	Private Service No.8180
Birth:	1889 Titchfield, Hampshire
Death:	May 1915 Alexandria, Egypt
Home Address:	South Street, Titchfield
Next of Kin:	George Matthews

Charles was brought up in West Street and Church Street with siblings George and Annie. When Charles was six their mother Harriett died and their father married again. Both brothers joined up as regular recruits with the 2nd battalion of the Hampshire Regiment, Charles in February 1908. They were based in Mauritius and India in the years before war broke out.

Recalled back to Europe, the convoy of around 900 men reached Plymouth on the 'Gloucester Castle', before joining the 88th Brigade, 29th Division. They were then dispatched to Gallipoli, via Malta on 28th March 1915 as part of the Mediterranean Expeditionary Force, to capture the strategic Gallipoli Peninsular from enemy forces. The Gallipoli Peninsula in Turkey forms one side of the Dardanelles Strait, an historic waterway that links the Black and the Aegean Seas. Cape Helles lies at the southernmost tip of the peninsula, an inhospitable area with steep sided hills.

On 25th April the 29th Division fought their way ashore at Cape Helles and over the next three weeks there was a constant push towards the Turkish lines. Between 20th and 24th May a suspension of hostilities was negotiated to allow both sides to retrieve the injured and bury the dead. By the 25th Private Matthews had already been injured and evacuated by ship to Alexandria hospital where he died of his injuries. He is buried in Chatby Military & War Memorial Cemetery in Eygpt. His elder brother George survived the war and lived in Bellfield, Titchfield until his death in 1954.

By the end of the war, the total casualties for the 29th Division were 94,000, its members had won 27 Victoria Crosses, including 12 at Gallipoli and it had become known as the 'Immortal 29th Division'.

2nd Battalion Hampshire Regiment

Private Matthews (centre) circa 1912

WILLIAM THOMAS MATHEWS

Service:	14th Battalion Hampshire Regiment
Rank:	Corporal Service No.15078
Birth:	1885 Titchfield, Hampshire
Death:	3rd Sep 1916 Beaumont-Hamel, France
Home Address:	Church Path, Titchfield
Next of Kin:	William & Harriet Mathews (nee Fleet)

William was the oldest of seven children of William, a jobbing gardener and his wife Harriet. William junior was a labourer for hire, living at home until he enlisted into the 14th Battalion Hampshire (1st Portsmouth Pals) Regiment in Gosport, alongside his neighbour Henry Edmunds. After extensive training the regiment proceeded to France, as part of the 39th Division, landing at Le Havre on the 6th March 1916.

Corporal Mathew's experience in August and September of 1916 will have been similar to that of fellow Titchfield lad Henry John Edmunds during the final push into German trenches north of Hamel on the Somme.

Sometime that day Corporal William Thomas Mathews was registered as 'missing' and he is one of the 72,000 men commemorated on the Thiepval Memorial which states

> *"Here are recorded names of officers and men of the British Armies who fell on the Somme battlefields between July 1915 and March 1918 but to whom the fortune of war denied the known and honoured burial given to their comrades in death."*

Beyond the Memorial

14th Service Battalion with William among the faces, taken behind the Great Hall Winchester (Paul Reed, Great War Photos)

Percy George Merritt

Service:	Royal Navy Submarine E3
Rank:	Petty Officer Stoker Service No.301550
Birth:	20th Mar 1885 Bishops Waltham, Hampshire
Death:	18th Oct 1914 off Borkum Island, North Sea
Home Address:	Bridge Street, Titchfield
Next of Kin:	Sybil Lucy Merritt (nee Matthews)

PO Merritt was one of seven children to Charles, a domestic coachman and his wife Deborah Miles, brought up in Fleet End, Warsash. He married Sybil Matthews in 1909 and had three children, Percy William in 1910, Sybil Agnes in 1912, and Dorothy Rosalie in 1914. They lived at 12 Bridge Street, now known as Keg Cottage. Percy joined the Navy on 2nd September 1902 initially on ships for seven years, becoming a leading stoker and then Petty Officer on submarines. As is traditional in the British Navy he had a tattoo on his right forearm, his of a Japanese lady.

Submarine E3 sailed from Harwich on 16th October 1914 to patrol off an island called Borkum in the North Sea. They spotted German destroyers and laid low in an island bay until they had passed. Unfortunately for E3 the German submarine U-27 was also patrolling near Borkum and saw E3. U-27 tracked the British submarine for two hours before unleashing two torpedoes which sank E3 immediately with the loss of all 28 crew. U27 saw four men in the water shortly after the attack, but when they returned to the scene half an hour later, there was no sign.

E3 was the first UK submarine to be sunk in the war and was the first ever fatal attack on one submarine by another. Mrs Sybil Merritt became Titchfield's first war widow.

Percy's two brothers were also in the Navy and killed in action. Walter

Harry was killed on HMS Good Hope (see George Ford) in the Battle of Coronel on 1st November 1914, age 30. Wilfred Howard was killed in action on HMS Invincible in the Battle of Jutland on 31st May 1916, age 23. The eldest brother Frederick Charles joined the army and survived.

The wreck of E3 was discovered by Dutch divers in 1994, four days short of 80 years after its loss.

Percy early on in his naval career

Titchfield Remembers Project

Bridge Street with 12 Bridge Street in the distance

Keg Cottage as it looks now

Arthur Newby

Service:	15th Battalion Hampshire Regiment
Rank:	Private Service No.20620
Birth:	1894 Titchfield, Hampshire
Death:	7th Oct 1916 Somme, France
Home Address:	West Street, Titchfield
Next of Kin:	Edith Burgess formally Newby (nee Cross Veck)

Arthur was the youngest of Frederick and Edith's six sons; all six fought in WWI, but only four returned. Frederick senior was a labourer who died just before Arthur was born and so the boys were brought up by their stepfather David Burgess. Arthur was working as a fruit grower by the time he was 17, and at 21 he joined the 15th (2nd Portsmouth Pals) Battalion of the Hampshire Regiment. After training they joined 122nd Brigade, 41st Division and by early May 1916 they left for France. That autumn they were in action at The Battle of Flers-Courcelette in September where the 122nd, despite losing 1,200 out of 1,800 men, captured the village.

"The last days of September 1916 were marked by heavy rain, which became even heavier and more continuous during the first days of October. The countless shell-holes became slimy pools; the churned soil of the Somme ridges melted into knee-deep mud, which made movement more and more difficult" 'Worcestershire Regiment WWI History' by Captain H. Fitz M. Stacke, M.C.

The bombardment began at 7 a.m. on 1st October along the entire Fourth Army front, the first day of the Battle of the Transloy Ridges and at 3.15pm the infantry went in. The attack met fierce German resistance and it was not until the afternoon of 3rd that the objectives were secured including the 41st division capturing Eaucourt L'Abbaye. The follow-up attack was delayed by worsening weather, only starting at 1.45pm on 7th October. The 41st advanced towards Butte de Warlencourt, an ancient burial mound and towards their ultimate objective, Ligny Thilloy.

Arthur died during the advance towards the village of Ligny Thilloy on the afternoon of 7th October. His elder brother Frederick was killed eight months later.

Arthur's sacrifice is commemorated at the Thiepval Memorial Somme France (c) Linge

Frederick Newby

Service:	1st Battalion Hampshire Regiment
Rank:	Private Service No. 25035
Birth:	1883 Titchfield, Hampshire
Death:	23rd Jun 1917 Arras, France
Home Address:	The Harris, Titchfield
Next of Kin:	Emily Mabel Newby (nee Whitmore)

Frederick was the eldest of six sons, who all fought in the First World War. He worked as a domestic gardener and later a market gardener before he married Emily Whitmore in 1906. In 1909 Edith Mercia was born and the family were living in The Harris, a small group of Titchfield cottages off East Street.

Frederick joined the 1st Hampshire Regiment as a regular sometime after 1911, and as part of the 4th Division, 11th Brigade, they were despatched to France on the 23rd August 1914. They headed for the Western Front as part of the Third Army under the command of General Edmund Allenby. On Christmas Day 1914, men of the 1st Battalion participated in the legendary Christmas truce where British and German soldiers fraternised in no man's land. The 1st Hampshires fought at Ypres in 1915 and the Somme in 1916.

The purpose of the Arras Offensive was to attack the enemy stronghold known as the Hindenburg Line, a German defensive position built during the winter of 1916/1917. It was, in terms of loss of life, the most costly British offensive of the war. It started on the 9th April 1917 and went on until mid-May, with a large-scale attack on 3rd May, now called The Third Battle of Scarpe, a terrible day for the British Army with a daily casualty rate higher than the Somme. Haig instructed the commanders of Third and Fifth Army to simultaneously resume the offensive on that day, with the Third Army to take the Scarpe valley and make another attempt on Roeux. The British commanders along a 13 mile front couldn't agree on a start time; a compromise was reached, but the Third Army needed longer to achieve their objectives and so were disadvantaged by the later start time. Disorganised from the start, many units had no idea which direction to attack.

The 4th Division were again in the front line on 11th May with a sixth and final attack on Roeux. The Battle of Arras officially ended on 17th May and sometime during the offensive private Frederick Newby was injured. It is likely that he was evacuated to the 42nd Casualty Clearing Station where he died of his wounds.

Frederick was buried in Aubigny-en-artois Cemetery France

Ernest Edward Pharoah

Service:	23rd Heavy Battery Royal Garrison Artillery
Rank:	Gunner Service No.66486
Birth:	1893 Titchfield, Hampshire
Death:	16th Oct 1917 Lijssenthoek, Belgium
Home Address:	Whiteley Pastures Farm, Titchfield
Next of Kin:	George & Mary Pharoah (nee Hunt)

Ernest was one of fourteen children born to George, a local farmer, and his wife Mary. Ernest's role as a young lad on Whiteley Pastures Farm was working with cattle, before his enlisted at Gosport and became a gunner.

Before the Great War a Heavy Battery was allocated to each infantry division and so in 1914 many went to war with those divisions. They were equipped with 60 pounder (5 inch) guns firing large calibre high explosive shells to neutralise the enemy artillery and destroy roads and railways behind enemy lines.

Heavy artillery brigades were then formed, being deployed wherever they were needed. It was only just after Gunner Pharoahs' death that the situation stabilized and that these batteries were permanently assigned to a particular brigade for the remainder of the war.

The Third Battle of Ypres consisted of several battles and represented the major British offensive on the Western Front in 1917. The goals included disrupting the German railway supply lines and the occupation of the Belgium coast and both these required taking and holding the high ground at Ypres.

Field Marshal Herbert Plumer's success at Messines Ridge in June marked the opening of the campaign; he then became head of the 'Second Army' which included the 23rd Heavy Battery. Fighting resumed in late September, an autumn that saw torrential rain, the beginning of the kind of muddy morass that has come to epitomise trench warfare. The Second Army was responsible for The Battle of Poelcappelle on 9th October 1917 and The First Battle of Passchendaele three days later, both failing in their objectives due to terrible weather and the inability to supply required artillery.

By the end of the 12th October, the high ground around Passchendaele remained in German hands and resulted in a huge number of British casualties. One of those wounded that day was Gunner Ernest Pharoah. He would have been transferred from a nearby dressing station to the clearing station at Lijssenthoek, a hospital since 1914.

Ernest died four days later and is buried at the Lijssenthoek Military Cemetery on the hospital site, the second largest Commonwealth Cemetery in Belgium, among 10,755 casualties of the First World war. Unusually almost all servicemen's graves are identified here, as most were wounded coming from the front with their dog tags and personal possessions in place.

Three of his brothers, Andrew, George and Wilfred also fought in the First World War and survived. The Pharoah family were still farming at nearby Funtley in the 1930's.

Titchfield Remembers Project

Wilf, Percy, Owen, Len, Bertie
Ethel, Andrew, Mary, George, Mary, George, Edith
Chris, Olive, Earnest

The Pharoah family with Ernest lying on the ground bottom right

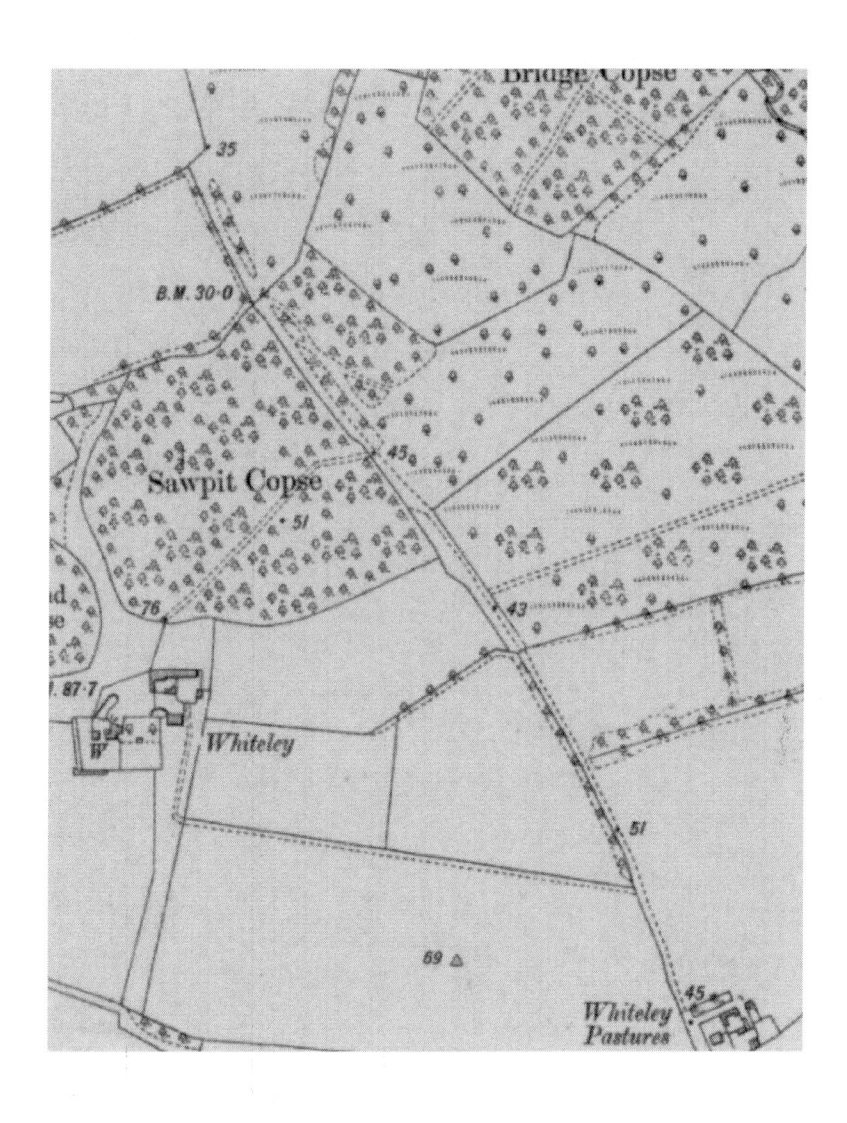

Location of the Whiteley Pastures Farm, of which nothing remains.

Duncan Phelps

Service:	2nd Battalion Royal Sussex, Hants Yeo. & 15th Hants
Rank:	2nd Lieutenant Service No.754 100086 & 204831
Birth:	1887 Fareham, Hampshire
Death:	29th Sep 1918 Ypres Belgium
Home Address:	Stonehaven, 53 Southampton Road
Next of Kin:	Sydney & Theodosia Phelps (nee Mace)

Duncan Phelps was one of five children brought up in the Parish of Emsworth, moving to Titchfield at the turn of the century. By 1911 Duncan was working as an Estate Agents Clerk and boarding at a house on the Southampton Road. His three older brothers were not called up; one of them, Ralph, continued to run the Portland Pub in Fareham.

The 2nd Battalion of the Royal Sussex Regiment crossed the channel with the British Expeditionary Force in 1914. It was during the first Battle of Ypres that they were given the unofficial title "The Iron Regiment" as an unsolicited testimonial by German prisoners.

Duncan Phelps was seconded to Hampshire Yeomanry on 17th January 1917 and sent for infantry training. He was 'commissioned in the field' on 28th May, promoted to 2nd Lieutenant. They were in action during the advance in Flanders, including the capture of Ploegsteert and Hill 63, before 12 officers and 307 men were re-organised into the 15th Battalion (2nd Portsmouth), Hampshire Regiment on 27th September 1917 as part of the 122nd Brigade, 41st Division of the Third Army, where they saw action at the Somme and Ypres.

The Advance in Flanders took place throughout September 1918. The Official War Diary states that after particularly fierce fighting on the 4th September and there were further assaults throughout the month.

Beyond the Memorial

"Burying parties" were sent out on the 15th, 16th and 17th September and there is a page at the end of the month listing officer's names that were wounded or killed. 2nd Lieutenant Phelps is not mentioned, but was missing presumed dead.

His war started and ended at Ypres.

On the 29th September Bulgaria signed an armistice and with defeat imminent, the German Kaiser agreed shortly after to end the war.

(C) CWGC Duncan is remembered on the Tyne Cot Memorial, Belgium, alongside 34,948 others.

Arthur Price

Service:	1st/8th Middlesex Regiment
Rank:	Private Service No.7640
Birth:	1890 Titchfield, Hampshire
Death	2nd Feb 1917 Nord, France
Home Address:	Hook Gate, Titchfield Common
Next of Kin:	Tom & Kate Price (nee Gale)

Son of a farm labourer, Arthur was brought up first in Bridge Street with eight siblings, later moving to Hook. He joined the Hampshire Special Reserve (Territorial) in 1910, these part-time home defence soldiers were nicknamed 'Saturday Night Soldiers'.

In 1911 Arthur applied to join the Shropshire Regiment, but by April he was training with the 1st Hampshire's in Aldershot. Sometime later he moved across to the 1st/8th Battalion, the Middlesex Regiment (Duke of Cambridge's Own) also known as the Die-Hards. In 1916 they became part of the 167th Brigade in the newly reformed 56th (London) Division.

At the battle of the Somme on 1st July 1916 the 56th Division was used as part of a diversionary tactic designed to confuse the enemy as to the true location of the Somme advance. *"Unpleasant as it may seem, the role of the 56th Division was to induce the enemy to shoot at them with as many guns as could be gathered together."* (Divisional Historian)

Casualties were 182 officers and 4,567 men killed, wounded or missing, a staggering loss of life to gain a mere seven miles.

The winter of 1916/17 in the Somme was the hardest of the war, with freezing conditions, heavy snow and little action. By the 1st January 1917 the 1st/8th Middlesex as part of the Third Army were in the old Neuve

Chapelle trenches twelve miles west of Arras awaiting the order to push back the German Hindenburg line.

Private Price died on the 2nd February 1917, killed presumably by one of the arbitrary rifle rounds across no man's land *"Quiet day spent in the trenches casualties see Lieut. H.S. Bainton wounded, killed other rks 1 wounded 2 very cold"*. Official War Diary.

Arthur is buried at Pont du Hem Cemetery, in what had previously been an apple orchard.

JOHN FRANK PRICE

Service:	7th Battalion Border Regiment
Rank:	Private Service No.39433
Birth:	1891 Titchfield, Hampshire
Death:	4th Nov 1918 France
Home Address:	Fairthorne Cottages, Catisfield
Next of Kin:	John & Mary Eliza Price (nee Child)

John Frank grew up with his family in Catisfield, son of a harness maker turned baker. His older brother William was a marine, his younger brother Geoffrey saw active service in the 15th Hussars in France in 1915 and survived the war.

John Frank served with the Army Service Corps before joining the 7th Battalion of the Border Regiment. This was formed in Carlisle, moving later to train in Andover and then to Winchester in 1915. In September 1917 it absorbed the Westmoreland and Cumberland Yeomanry and was renamed the 7th (Westmoreland and Cumberland) Battalion. The 7th battalion was in the 51st Brigade, 17th (Northern) Division, which in turn was part of the Third Army.

The Battle of the Sambre took place in the final advance. By November 1918 the old trench system was collapsing and it was now open warfare between the two armies. The Germans resorted to using geographical features to defend and on 4th November 1918 it was the Sambre-Oise canal within the dense forest of Mormal.

This last major offensive was launched just before dawn on a typical cloudy day with the British First, Third and Fourth armies advancing north along the 30 mile front, with the Fourth Army focussed on breaching the canal. As they attempted this they came under heavy fire and there were many casualties before the temporary bridges were completed. One of those killed whilst trying to cross the canal under heavy enemy fire was the poet Wilfred Owen.

Meanwhile the 17th Division advanced through a belt of the densely wooded Forest of Mormal running west to east, about 2,000 yards wide, pushing forward for some four miles. The 51st Brigade, including the 7th Borders, took the centre, the 38th on its right and the 37th on its left. All three Brigades engaged in succession, on what was known as the "leap-frogging" plan. During this final assault Private Price was killed, just a week before the end of the war. On Armistice Day as the church bells were ringing in celebration of the end of the war to end all wars, Wilfred Owen's mother received the news of her son's death. As Titchfield's bells were ringing local families including Mr and Mrs Price were also counting the cost.

(C) CWGC John is buried in the Englefontaine British Cemetery in France.

Extract from Dulce Et Decorum Est (1917)
Wilfred Owen

Bent double, like old beggars under sacks,
Knock-kneed, coughing like hags, we cursed through sludge,
Till on the haunting flares we turned our backs,
And towards our distant rest began to trudge.
Men marched asleep. Many had lost their boots,
But limped on, blood-shod. All went lame, all blind;
Drunk with fatigue; deaf even to the hoots
Of gas-shells dropping softly behind.

Gas! GAS! Quick, boys! - An ecstasy of fumbling
Fitting the clumsy helmets just in time,
But someone still was yelling out and stumbling
And flound'ring like a man in fire or lime.-
Dim through the misty panes and thick green light,
As under a green sea, I saw him drowning.

Fairthorne Cottages Catisfield

WALTER REED

Service:	15th Battalion Hampshire Regiment
Rank:	Private Service No.20223
Birth:	1893 Locksheath, Hampshire
Death:	21st Jun 1917 Boulogne, France
Home Address:	Doris Dene, Titchfield Common
Next of Kin:	Thomas and Mary Ann Reed (nee Casey)

Walter was the youngest son of Thomas, a labourer and was brought up in Hunts Pond Road in the Parish of Titchfield.

He joined the 15th Battalion (2nd Portsmouth) in April 1915, one of Lord Kitchener's New Army recruits, known as the Portsmouth Pals. By October of that year they were attached to and training with the 122nd Brigade, 41st Division.

During the Somme Campaign, the Battle of Messines was fought between 7th and 14th June 1917, over the nine mile Messines Ridge which had been in German hands since 1914. This battle was the first substantial allied victory of the First World War, using all the Commonwealth forces; Australian & New Zealand Army Corps (Anzacs), Canadians, Irish and many of the British divisions. It was the first battle to employ the skills of all branches of the land forces, with tremendous success, putting into practice the lessons learned over the years of stalemate on the Western Front.

On the 7th June the main attack started with the detonation of over 450 tons of explosive placed in mines 75 feet deep below enemy lines along the front. Earth was sent skywards along a nine mile front stretching from the well known Hill 60 not far from Ypres, to an ancient farmstead close to the French Border. The explosion was heard along the coast of southern England. Opposition was minimal, as many enemy servicemen were too shocked to resist.

Sometime during this battle Private Walter Reed was wounded and was moved to a casualty clearing station on the coast where on the 21st June he died of his injuries. Walter is buried in the Boulogne Eastern Cemetery in France. A year later his elder brother Thomas died at the battle of Bethune. Both brothers are commemorated in Locksheath church.

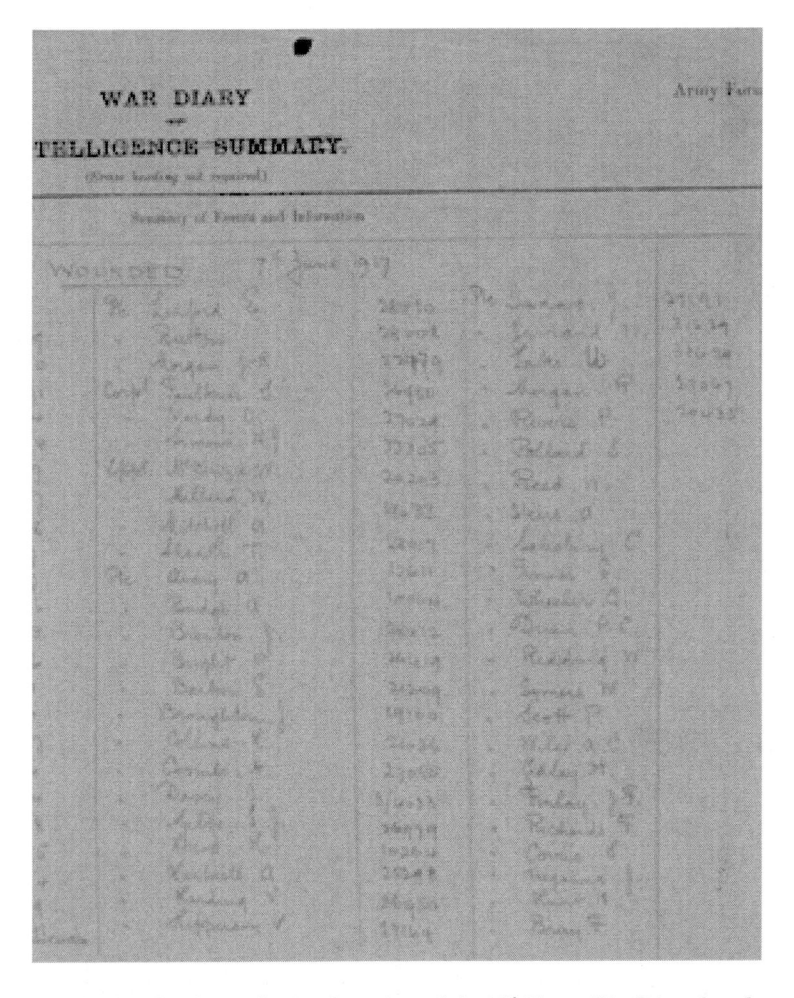

Unusually for official war diaries the writer of the 15th Hants War Diary has chosen to name all those killed or wounded on 21st June 1917 despite their rank.

William Sandy

Service:	2nd Battalion Hampshire Regiment
Rank:	Private Service No.8255
Birth:	1892 Titchfield, Hampshire
Death:	28th Apr 1915 Gallipoli, Turkey
Home Address:	West Street, Titchfield
Next of Kin:	William and Harriet Sandy (nee Gaywood)

The Sandy family were well established in Titchfield, going back several generations. They were agricultural labourers and later thatchers living in West Street when William and his siblings Thomas, Mary and Florence were born.

William joined the 2nd Battalion Hampshire Regiment, a regular battalion in 1914. After training he sailed on the 'Gloucester Castle' to Turkey to take part in the Gallipoli Campaign. He arrived on the 25th April 1915 at Cape Helles, with the 88th Brigade, 29th Division, along with his neighbour Private Charles Matthews.

Within two days the troops had disembarked and were on Gully Beach with kit and supplies. On the night of the 27th April orders were sent showing the plan for the following day. These were sketchy and did not allow time for the proper briefing of the frontline servicemen. At 08:00 hours on the 28th The First Battle of Krithia began. It included both French and British troops from different starting positions and a lack of artillery support which made maintaining a front line up the ravines a major task. Together with a misunderstanding concerning changes in direction, the line ground to a halt and troops simply dug in or retreated. The Turkish counter-attacked that night and forced the 88th Brigade to fall back and lose what ground they had won.

The British forces lost 2,000 men in their attempt to defeat the Turkish forces, one of those being Private Sandy, three days into his war.

William is one of 20,882 Commonwealth servicemen remembered on the Helles Memorial, Turkey, a 30 metre high obelisk commemorating Commonwealth servicemen who died and have no known grave.

Titchfield Remembers Project

WEST STREET, TITCHFIELD

An early image of West Street. The jettied houses at the bottom were deemed unfit for human habitation and demolished just before the Second World War. The Sandy family lived in the next house along in 1911.

JOHN SIMS

Service:	Royal Navy HMS Cressy
Rank:	Petty Officer Stoker Service No.148321
Birth:	14th Feb 1870 Meon, Titchfield
Death:	22nd Sep 1914 off Dutch Coast
Home Address:	Meon, Titchfield
Next of Kin:	Stephen and Ann Sims (nee Stone)

John Sims was one of ten children born between Titchfield and the Meon shore to Stephen Sims, an agricultural labourer and his wife Ann. In 1871 they were living at Little Posbrook with their young family. John joined the Royal Navy on 6th March 1889 and became a Petty Officer in 1910. He was assigned HMS Cressy, an old and slow armoured cruiser, in August 1914.

On the 22nd September 1914, three sister ships; HMS Aboukir, Hogue and Cressy were patrolling the North Sea off the coast of Holland. They had been at sea for two days with no enemy sighting and their escorting destroyers had been sent back to Harwich to refuel. At first light, the U9 submarine of the German Imperial Navy was patrolling the same area and had spotted the ships.

The report of the Admiralty of Commander Reginald A. Norton, late of H.M.S. Hogue, follows:

Between 6.15 and 6.30 a.m., H.M.S. Aboukir was struck by a torpedo. The Hogue closed on the Aboukir and I received orders to hoist out the launch, turn out and prepare all boats, and unlash all timber on the upper deck. Two lifeboats were sent to the Aboukir, but before the launch could get away the Hogue was struck on the starboard side amidships by two torpedoes at intervals of ten to twenty seconds. The ship at once began to heel to starboard.......

Commander Bertram W. L. Nicholson (H.M.S. Hogue)

Capt. Johnson then manoeuvred the ship [Cressy] so as to render assistance to the crews of the Hogue and Aboukir. About five minutes later another periscope was seen on our starboard quarter and fire was opened...... The ship listed about 10 degrees to the starboard and remained steady. The time was 7.15 a.m. A second torpedo fired by the same submarine missed and passed about 10 feet astern. About a quarter of an hour after the first torpedo had hit, a third torpedo fired from a submarine just before the starboard beam hit us under the No. 5 boiler room. The time was 7.30 a.m. The ship then began to heel rapidly, and finally turned keel up, remaining so for about twenty minutes before she finally sank, at 7.55 a.m.

A number of small vessels assisted in the rescue of survivors including a Lowestoft trawler 'L.T. Coriander' picked up 156 officers and men and two Dutch steamers 'Flora' and 'Titan' picked up more than 120. Each ship had a crew of around 750, a total of 1459 lost their lives of which 560 died on HMS Cressy, including John Sims.

The court of inquiry found fault with senior officers on all three ships for not patrolling in the usual zigzag method and the Admiralty for instigating such a dangerous patrol of little value.

Petty Officer Sims is commemorated in St. Peter's Titchfield, on panel 3 of the Portsmouth Naval Memorial and included in the De Ruvigny Roll of Honour.

Albert Ernest Smith

Service:	10th Battalion Hampshire Regiment
Rank:	Private Service No.14839
Birth:	1895 Titchfield, Hampshire
Death:	10th Aug 1915 Gallipoli, Turkey
Home Address:	Iron Mills Cottages, Titchfield
Next of Kin:	Albert and Rose Smith (nee Long)

Albert, the son of a railway worker, was working as an errand boy, before joining up to the 10th Hampshire Regiment, along with his neighbour Frank Biddle. They joined one of the newly formed service battalions at Winchester, as part of Kitcheners First Army in August 1914, and were attached to the 10th (Irish) Division. After training they sailed from Liverpool on 7th July 1915 and landed a month later on the Turkish coast.

With three fresh divisions of reinforcements promised to arrive in August by British war minister Lord Kitchener (increased to five); the Mediterranean Commander-in-Chief Sir Ian Hamilton began planning a major Allied offensive on the Gallipoli peninsular to coincide with their arrival.

The Battle of Gallipoli or The Dardanelles Campaign took place between 25th April 1915 and 9th January 1916 on the peninsula on the northern bank of the Dardanelles Strait. The strait provided a sea route to our Russian allies, so it was strategically important to gain control of the area.

Britain and France launched a naval attack followed by troop landings with the eventual aim of capturing the Ottoman capital of Constantinople, now called Istanbul. However, the Turks had received intelligence that attacks along the coast were planned and had amassed a considerable force.

The 6-7th August 1915 marked the second attempt to achieve the aims. The 10th Division landed and proceeded to make their way towards the front line, a scene of heavy shelling and continuous fighting, arriving 48 hours later at Chunuk Bair.

Sir Ian Hamilton's Third Gallipoli Despatch:

At daybreak on Tuesday, 10th August, the Turks delivered a grand attack from the line Chunuk Bair to Hill Q........ at 5.30 a.m., were assaulted by a huge column, consisting of no less than a full division plus a regiment of three battalions. [circa 5,000 men] *The Loyal North Lancashire men were simply overwhelmed in their shallow trenches by sheer weight in numbers, whilst the Wiltshires who were caught in the open, were literally almost annihilated. The ponderous mass of enemy swept over the crest, turned the right flank of our line below, swarmed round the Hampshires ....and were only extricated with great difficulty and very heavy losses. So far they* [29th Brigade] *had held on to all they had gained......... Unfortunately, these two pieces of ground, small and worthless as they seemed, were worth, according to the ethics of war, 10,000 lives, for by their loss or retention they just marked the difference between an important success and a signal victory.*

Private Albert Smith was 'killed in action' on the 10th August 1915, along with his neighbour Private Biddle. They had been in the war just five days.

*Iron Mills Cottages where three servicemen were brought up.
The cottages were demolished in 1963*

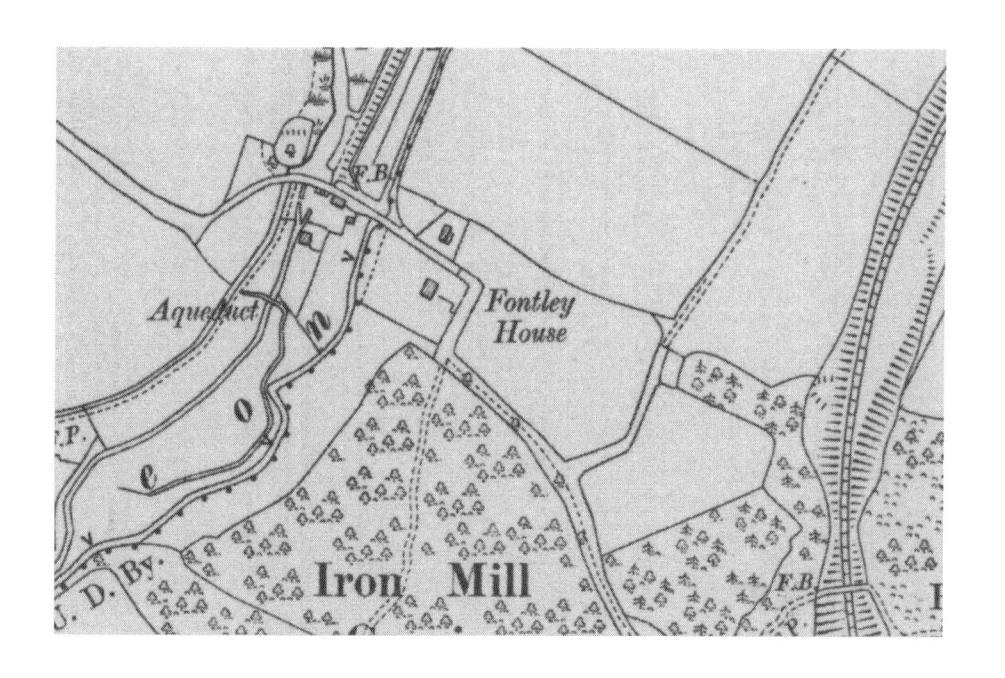

Location of Iron Mills between Titchfield and Funtley

CHARLES SMITH

Service:	1st/8th Hampshire Regiment (Isle of Wight Rifles)
Rank:	Rifleman Service No.37509
Birth:	1892 Titchfield, Hampshire
Death:	2nd Nov 1917 Gaza
Home Address:	May Cottage, Park Gate, Titchfield
Next of Kin:	Frederick and Ann Smith (nee Gregory)

Charlie Smith was one of eleven children of Frederick and Ann Smith. Frederick was a market gardener, who by 1911 had developed a local fruit growing business and his son Charlie aged 19 was working as a farm labourer.

Charlie joined up as a rifleman in 1914 with the 8th Hampshire Regiment, the Isle of Wight Rifles. They were also known as the "8th (Territorial) Battalion, Princess Beatrice's Isle of Wight Rifles", or the nickname "The Isle of Wight Ghurkhas" due to their dark green dress uniform and light infantry drill.

After time spent training they sailed from Liverpool on 30th July 1915 aboard the Aquitania, as part of the 163rd Infantry Brigade, 54th East Anglian Division bound for Gallipoli.

Initially fighting in Turkey, the division sailed to Alexandria, Giza and then on to the Suez Canal. In the first two months of 1917 they marched to Mazar and across the Sinai Desert, 145 miles in 12 days to El Arish.

The aim of the Egyptian Expeditionary Force (EEF) in the Sinai and Palestine Campaign was to defeat the Turkish Ottoman forces. Their defensive line between Beersheba and Gaza needed to be broken before moving on to Jerusalem and Syria *"as a Christmas present for the British people"* (David Lloyd George).

Issues such as the sourcing of enough water for men and horses and hot desert winds contributed to the first two battles of Gaza having been unsuccessful. In June 1917 a change of leadership revitalised the campaign. General Edmund Allenby set about improving the efficiency and morale of the EEF and encouraging irregular warfare practised by Colonel T. E. Lawrence (Lawrence of Arabia). The plan included using deception tactics, in the form of regular patrols towards enemy lines, in order to disguise a real attack.

The Third Battle of Gaza began with an artillery and naval bombardment for 72 hours followed by the moving into position of 47,500 infantry, 11,000 cavalry and 242 guns on the night of 30th October, ready for the attack on Beersheba. On the 1st and 2nd November the infantry including the 54th (East Anglia) carried out a series of coordinated assaults on Gaza's defences. This two stage attack succeeded in pushing back the Turkish lines west of Gaza, but at the cost of 2,700 casualties (350 dead, 340 missing and 2,000 wounded).

Rifleman Charlie Smith lost his life during this assault and is buried in the Gaza War Cemetery, Plot 21, Row B Grave 11.

Frank Smith

Service:	2nd Battalion Hampshire Regiment
Rank:	Private Service No.8728
Birth:	1893 Titchfield, Hampshire
Death:	11th Apr 1918 Somme, Belgium
Home Address:	West Street, Titchfield
Next of Kin:	Louisa Smith (nee Broomfield)

Frank Smith was one of twelve children of bricklayer David and his wife Eliza (nee Bedford) and was brought up in a cottage in West Street next to the Horse and Groom Public house. He first became a regular soldier in the 1st battalion of the Hampshire Regiment in 1910, when he turned 17. By 1914 Private Smith was in the 2nd Battalion and was later attached to the Military Foot Police. In the spring of 1915 he married Louisa Broomfield and within days he was heading for Gallipoli as part of the 88th Brigade, 29th Division. They retreated from Turkey in January 1916 and were sent to the Somme, where they fought with the Second Army at the Battles of Albert and Transloy Ridges. 1917 saw involvement in both the Arras and Ypres Offensives and finally the Battle of the Lys in the final year of the war.

On 21st March 1918 the German Spring Offensive on the Western Front started as massive gun battle in an attempt to end the war. In just five hours, the enemy fired one million artillery shells at the British lines and this bombardment was followed by elite storm troopers, travelling light and moving quickly. Unused to this tactic, 21,000 British soldiers were taken prisoner on day one and the remaining troops withdrew. The Germans had made great advances, but soon experienced a major problem. The speed of their advance put their supply lines under huge strain and those leading the attack became short of both sustenance and ammunition.

On 9th April the enemy tried again with a smaller offensive south of Ypres, which captured the Messines Ridge and much of the Passchendaele Salient. Once again the German push lost forward momentum and with troops desperate for food, discipline broke down. Though the German attack had been spectacular in terms of land conquered, it had also been expensive in terms of men lost. Between March and April, the German Army had 230,000 casualties; they simply could not sustain such numbers. Between March and July 1918, the Germans lost one million men.

Military Records report Private Frank Smith as 'presumed dead' on 11th April 1918. His body was never identified.

Frank is commemorated on the Ploegsteert Memorial, Belgium. (c) CWGC

FRANK SIDNEY SMITH

Service:	10th Battalion Hampshire Regiment
Rank:	Private Service No.10126
Birth:	1896 Titchfield, Hampshire
Death:	21st Aug 1915 Gallipoli, Turkey
Home Address:	Segensworth Farm, Titchfield
Next of Kin:	Alfred and Annie Smith

Frank Sidney was one of seven children born into a family of farm labourers who, for generations, lived on the outskirts of the village. When not working on the land, father Alfred was a platelayer for the local railway working alongside his twin Albert. Frank Sidney was working as a farm servant, before he enlisted in the Hampshire Regiment on the 27th April 1915, with his cousin Albert. After training as part of the 10th Irish Division, 29th Brigade they left from Liverpool and landed on the coast of Turkey on the 6th August.

The Gallipoli campaign had started on the 25th April and was an attempt knock Germany's ally Turkey out of the war. The plan was to land troops on the peninsular and make their way to the capital Constantinople. General Sir Ian Hamilton, the commander of the Mediterranean Expeditionary Forces decided on one final push to secure this objective to enable his troops to move from the beaches to the high ground. To improve the chances of success he removed some of the commanding officers, but despite changes of command the battle for Scimitar Hill on the 21st August 1915 was another catastrophe.

Between the fierce retaliation by the Turks and the ensuing fires in the surrounding bushes, in one day of fighting the British suffered 5,300 casualties out of the 14,300 soldiers who participated. Frank Sidney

Smith, at war for only 15 days was among those killed and his life is commemorated on the Helles Memorial, Turkey. He was the last of six Titchfield men to die in the campaign. An evacuation of the remaining troops took place three months later.

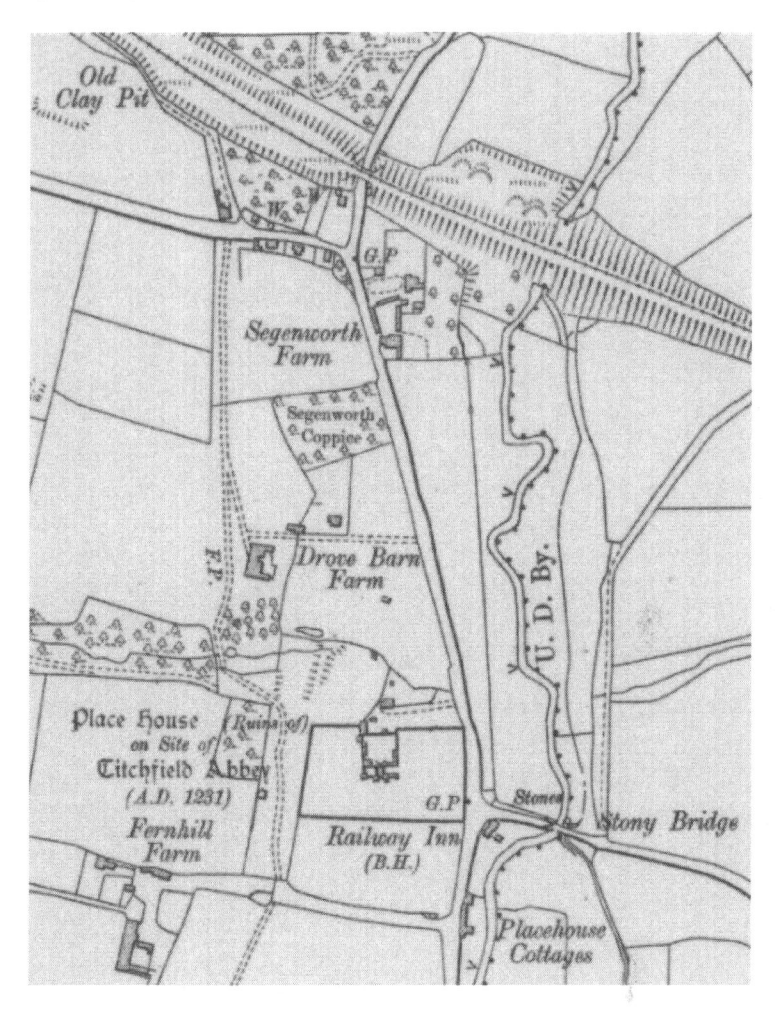

Location of the family farm at Segensworth Titchfield

WALTER GEORGE SMITH

Service: 41st Coy/11th Battalion Royal Army Ordnance Corps

Rank: Private   Service No. 6/1139 (Training Reserve)

Birth: 1884 Titchfield, Hampshire

Death: 2nd Dec 1916 Rugeley Camp, Staffordshire

Home Address: West Street, Titchfield

Next of Kin: Lillian Smith (nee Rogers)

Walter grew up in Church Path and West Street with his parents David and Eliza Smith (nee Bedford) and eleven siblings. He became a farm labourer and in 1912 married Lillian Rogers. Just before war broke out Lillian gave birth to Dorothy who died a year later.

He enlisted with The Royal Army Ordnance Corps and was fully trained by 20th January 1915. The RAOC was the body responsible for supplying weapons, ammunition and equipment to the British Army and in addition new recruits needed to be trained on how to use those weapons. Private Smith was then stationed at the Rugeley Camp, Cannock Chase in Staffordshire as part of the Training Reserve. Rugeley Camp and its neighbour Brocton were firstly used as transit camps for onward battalions heading to the Western Front; the camps were later used for training, even building practice trenches. They were capable of holding up to 40,000 men and trained approximately 500,000. The camps were fully equipped small villages with their own church, post office and a bakery. With many servicemen in close proximity illness and disease was common. During WWI at Rugeley there were numerous epidemics of spotted fever recorded (Meningococcal Meningitis) and other common infections.

Private Walter Smith died at the Rugeley Camp Military Hospital in Staffordshire aged 32 and is buried there.

Walter's youngest brother Frank of the 2nd Hampshire's died on 11th April 1918. He is also remembered in this book.

Walter's grave at Rugeley Camp Cemetery Staffordshire. (Image M.Brennand)

Frank Stuart

Service:	1st Battalion Duke of Cornwall Light Infantry
Rank:	Rifleman Service No.41274 (formally 8/7385 Reservist)
Birth:	1899 Westminster, London
Death:	1st Aug 1918 Bapaume, France
Home Address:	South Street, Titchfield
Next of Kin:	John & Lucy Stuart (nee Wyatt)

Frank Stuart, his parents and his two sisters were visiting their Grandmother Charlotte Wyatt on the night of 31st March 1901 when the census enumerator called at her house in South Street, Titchfield. His father John was a retired member of the London Police Force and was clearly unwell as within weeks he had died. His mother Lucy then took on a housekeeper's job in a mansion block in London and the children were split up.

Frank moved to the Metropolitan & City Police Orphanage in Twickenham and his two sisters went to their Grandmother's in South Street, Titchfield. At 16 Frank joined the Territorial Force, a form of part-time volunteer soldiering designed to provide home defence. Frank enlisted with the 13th Reserve Battalion Hampshire Regiment, which spent the early years of the war on the south coast under the Exeter based line of Reserve Regiments, finally becoming the 34th Training Reserve. By late 1916 general mobilisation called upon all reservists and Frank was transferred to the DCLI 14th Infantry Brigade, 5th Division and spent his first few months in Italy. By March 1918 the division was in France and fought in the Battle of Lys. After two weeks rest playing sports (winning at cricket but losing at football) they were recalled back to the front.

The Second Battle of Bapaume started on a misty morning on the 21st August. It was to be the turning point of the First World War on the Western Front and the beginning of what was later known as the Allies'

Hundred Days Offensive. Improved armoured support and artillery bombardment had weakened once impregnable positions and helped the allies break through. The enemy trenches were captured with a human loss considerably less than other battles.

"Assembly complete at 2pm 31st inst. The Brigade was ordered to attack and capture the enemy's position..... There was no preliminary bombardment but the guns opened fire with a creeping barrage... The mist was so thick that nothing could be seen after about 70 yards...Casualties in our Battalion were extremely light (2 officers and 50 other ranks)" Extracts from the 1st Battalion War Diary

Sometime during this offensive Rifleman Stuart was killed, but his body was not found.

Frank is remembered on the Vis-en-Artois Memorial just outside Arras.

Titchfield Remembers Project

Young Frank in his Territorial uniform

Plaque at the Metropolitan & City Police Orphanage

Victor George Taylor

Service:	2nd Battalion Royal Berkshire Regiment
Rank:	Lance Corporal Service No.27498
Birth:	1891 Portsmouth, Hampshire
Death:	27th Aug 1916 Vermelles, France
Home Address:	Milton, Portsmouth
Next of Kin:	Frederick & Mary Taylor (nee Holmes)

Victor George Taylor was brought up at The Victoria Hotel in Surrey Street Portsmouth with three siblings, Frederick, Ethel and Thomas. Victor was a regular soldier, having enlisted first, at 18 in the 2nd Battalion of the Royal Worcester Regiment and then in the Royal Berkshire 2nd Battalion by 1914. Sometime later he also was engaged with the Army Cycling Corps.

At the outbreak of war the 2nd Battalion's of both the Worcestershires and Berkshires were in India. They returned home.

The 2nd Berkshires joined the 25th Brigade in Winchester for training and landed at Le Havre on 5th November 1914. The next three months were spent in the trenches. They suffered terribly from trench foot and other illnesses caused by the abrupt change of climate. Nicknamed 'The Biscuit Boys', as their barracks were near Huntley & Palmers factory, 'suppliers of biscuits to the army', the Berkshire Regiment served on the Western Front throughout the conflict, taking part in the 'Christmas Truce' in that first winter of the war.

On the 28th March 1916 the Regiment was moved to the Somme area, as part of the build up for the coming offensive. Towards the end of June a scouting party made a silent reconnaissance on the enemy trenches and found the Germans content in their deep dugouts despite constant artillery bombardment. The party reported their findings to higher authority, but were told they were mistaken. This error of judgement was to have a profound effect on the casualty numbers in the coming weeks.

1st July 1916 at The Battle of Albert, on the first day of the Somme offensive the 8th Division lost over 5,000 men. Of the 20,000 British killed that day, Corporal Taylor survived to continue fighting.

The Battle of Delville Wood, 15th July to 3rd September, was one of the bloodiest confrontations of the Somme, with both sides incurring many casualties. Whilst it is considered a tactical allied victory, this victory should be measured against the huge losses sustained. The 2nd Battalion were in the front line trenches near Sailly La Borse by the middle of August. Although the official War Diary does not give details of the engagements there are regular lists of casualties from the 16th to the 27th. On the 27th it reads

"In TRENCHES. Flank Battalions 2nd RIFLE BRIGADE on right flank, 2nd LINCOLN REGT on left flank. Draft of 6 other ranks joined Battalion. 2 men wounded, 3 men to hospital."

The list included Corporal Taylor who died from his injuries.

By the time plans were underway for the memorial Victor's parents had moved to High Street, Titchfield.

The grave of Victor George Taylor at Vermelles Military Cemetery near Bethune, France.

Victor (31) and brother Thomas (32) running in either the Portsmouth Harriers or Beagles around 1908

Donald Barfoot Edwards Upshall

Service:	1st Battalion Northumberland Fusiliers
Rank:	Fusilier Service No.3720
Birth:	1895 Broughton, Hampshire
Death:	9th Apr 1917 Arras, France
Home Address:	School House, West Street, Titchfield
Next of Kin:	William & Sarah Emma Upshall (nee Petty)

Donald was one of five siblings, whose father was a schoolmaster first at the Endowed Boys School in Broughton and then at the Schoolhouse at the top of West Street in Titchfield. Donald joined the army in 1913 and so like many of the Titchfield lads he was a regular soldier and one of the first to leave for France in 1914.

With the Regimental Motto 'Quo Fata Vocant' 'Wherever the Fates Call" the Northumberland Fusiliers raised 52 battalions, more than any other Regiment and were awarded five Victoria Crosses.

The 1st Battalion was stationed at Portsmouth as part of the 9th Brigade of the 3rd Division. They mobilised for war on the 14th August, landing at La Havre and engaged in the major actions on the Western Front as part of the Third Army.

The Battle of Arras - the First Battle of the Scarpe 9th -14th April was one of the relatively few cavalry actions that took place in the First World War bringing to mind the film & stage play 'War Horse'.

Anxious to avoid repeating the costly mistakes of Verdun and the Somme the previous year, a cunning plan was hatched whereby New Zealand engineers would create a vast underground network of tunnels through which the troops could pass to come up directly in front of the German front line without having to face machine gun fire in no man's land. Large scale models were built to help officers understand the landscape and rehearsals were staged. Harbouring no illusions about the battle to come, the British Army also installed a well equipped hospital capable of treating 700 wounded. By the end of March over 11 miles of tunnels had been completed, the largest ever undertaken by the British Army. On the eve of the Battle of Arras the caves and quarries under the town contained more than 24,000 soldiers; one of them was Fusilier Donald Upshall. On 6th April troop morale was given a major boost when the announcement was made that the United States was entering the war. On Easter Monday 9th April 1917 at 5.30 a.m. during a snowstorm, the Canadian & British army's advanced, capturing most of the 5 mile ridge.

During this first day's offensive Donald Upshall lost his life and is remembered on the Arras Memorial, France

The Arras Memorial

The Arras Memorial commemorates 35,000 British soldiers who died and have no known grave.

The General (1917)
Edward Thomas

The flowers left thick at nightfall in the wood
This Eastertide call into mind the men,
Now far from home, who, with their sweethearts, should
Have gathered them and will do never again.
'Good-morning; good-morning!' the General said
When we met him last week on our way to the line.
Now the soldiers he smiled at are most of 'em dead,
And we're cursing his staff for incompetent swine.
'He's a cheery old card,' grunted Harry and Jack
As they slogged up to Arras with rifle and pack.
But he did for them both by his plan of attack.

2nd/Lieut Thomas RGA died 9th April 1917 Arras

BENJAMIN WATERFALL

Service:	Royal Navy HMS Research
Rank:	Chief Petty Officer Service No.151119
Birth:	10th Apr 1876 Deptford, Greenwich, London
Death:	14th Mar 1917 Portland, Dorset
Home Address:	West Street, Titchfield
Next of Kin:	Matilda Ann Waterfall (nee Frampton)

Benjamin Waterfall was the second of nine children of Benjamin, an engine driver from Deptford and Christiana Porter from Reading. He joined the Navy on 17th August 1889, his service papers clearly document his career through the ships on which he served and medals won and on 1st June 1909 he became a Petty Officer. He married Matilda in 1899 and started married life in West Street Titchfield where their girls, Annie, Emily and Minnie were born and later moved to 28 Winstanley Road, Portsmouth and had Benjamin James.

During WWI CPO Waterfall, already entitled to retire, was stationed on shore firstly at the Gunnery training School HMS Excellent and then HMS Victory. Finally at HMS Research at Portland, an old RN paddle-steamer used as a depot ship for locally employed armed trawlers engaged in minesweeping. Although it is not known when he contracted tuberculosis, it may have been the reason for his shore based employment at the end of his long naval career. He died at Portland Naval Hospital and is buried in St. Peter's graveyard Titchfield, Hampshire.

Beyond the Memorial

St. Peters Churchyard, Titchfield, Hampshire

Chief Petty Officer Waterfall

149

Francis Edward Watts

Service:	Royal Navy HMS Black Prince
Rank:	Petty Officer 1st Class (Sailmaker) Service No.188210
Birth:	27th Mar 1881 Clanfield, Oxfordshire
Death:	31st May 1916 off Jutland, Denmark
Home Address:	Crosswell House, High Street, Titchfield
Next of Kin:	Elsie May Watts (nee Watts)

Francis Edward Watts was the seventh of thirteen children to John Watts, a farmer from Oxfordshire and Rebecca Watts who was brought up on a Whiteley farm just outside Titchfield.

In the 1830's one branch of the Oxfordshire Watts moved to Hampshire and Francis married into this, his Mother's side, of the family in 1908. He and Elsie May, a farmer's daughter from Whiteley set up home at Crosswell House Upper High Street Titchfield. They had two children Francis in 1908 and Arthur in 1910.

By lying on his enlistment papers Francis began his naval training at 15 on HMS St. Vincent, the permanently moored training ship at Gosport and became a fully fledged seaman on 27th March 1898. Whilst large naval vessels no longer relied on sails, Sail makers at this time were employed on all tasks relating to stitching canvas and this would have included awnings, hammocks and maintaining sails for the small auxiliary communication craft used in harbour.

HMS Black Prince was sunk at the Battle of Jutland, but her end was a mystery for many years. During WWI the British fleet were using visual signals by flags, semaphore and morse by signal lamp to transmit orders such as changes of course. This meant that during periods of poor visibility, at night or at a distance between ships, these methods were ineffective. It is believed, through the study of German records that HMS

Black Prince, (during the evening of 31st May), once separated from the First Cruiser Squadron, sailed towards the German fleet. Having discovered his error, Rear Admiral Sir Robert Arburthnot immediately changed course but was still in close range when several German ships opened fire. Black Prince was hit by around twelve heavy shells and several smaller ones and sank within 15 minutes close to midnight on 31st May 1916. In the dark freezing waters of the North Sea all her 857 crew were lost.

Portsmouth Memorial

Titchfield Remembers Project

East Street image around 1930 showing Crosswell House facing the camera at the end

Arthur Carnarvon Whittaker

Service:	1st Battalion Hampshire Regiment
Rank:	Private Service No.33461
Birth:	1899 Titchfield, Hampshire
Death:	22nd Mar 1918 Pozieres, France
Home Address:	Southampton Hill, Titchfield
Next of Kin:	Carnarvon and Kate Whittaker (nee Powell)

Arthur was the elder child of Carnarvon, a merchant seaman and his wife Kate. Initially a Trooper in the part-time Territorial Force, The Hampshire Yeomanry Arthur joined the 1st Hampshire Regiment sometime in 1917 when he turned 18.

By March 1918 a major German offensive had been expected for many months and when Russia withdrew from the war, it allowed the Germans to move forty-four divisions of men to the Western Front. With America now in the war, Germany wanted to make a move before the American forces arrived on the Somme.

The 1st Hampshires were part of the 11th Brigade being prepared with both offensive and defensive training in readiness for the attack, which finally came on a foggy dawn on 21st March. By the end of the first day the Germans had advanced more than four miles and the British had nearly 20,000 dead and 35,000 wounded servicemen. Private Whittaker was one of the latter who succumbed to his injuries the following day, a year after his father was lost at sea.

Arthur is remembered here on the Pozieres Memorial, north-east of the town of Albert among 2,758 Commonwealth servicemen. The Memorial commemorates a further 14,300 men with no known grave.

CARNARVON LEWIS WHITTAKER

Service:	Merchant Marine SS Alnwick Castle
Rank:	Boatswain
Birth:	1861 Westbourne, Sussex
Death:	19th Mar 1917 due west of Isles of Scilly
Home Address:	Southampton Hill, Titchfield
Next of Kin:	Kate Whittaker (nee Powell)

Carnarvon Lewis was the second of four children to Richard, a Welsh outfitter and Matilda Watts, a shirt fitter from Fareham. He married Kate Powell in Fareham in 1897 and they had two sons, Reginald, who survived the war and Arthur who did not.

Bos'n Whittaker, a seasoned mariner, aged 53, was a senior crew member of the SS Alnwick Castle when the vessel was requisitioned to become a troop ship in August 1914. Once returned to its owners in 1917 she set sail on the 17th March from Plymouth bound for Cape Town, South Africa with one hundred crew, fourteen passengers and a cargo of silver. On the 18th, she picked up twenty-five survivors from the steamship 'Trevose', which had just been torpedoed by a German submarine.

At 6.10am the next morning the 'Alnwick Castle' was herself torpedoed, 310 miles off the Bishop Rock and within half an hour she had sunk. The u-boat came to the surface and trained her gun on the steamer, but as no shots were necessary to finish the job, she left without making contact. All crew and passengers took to the six boats and got safely away. But being 300 miles from the nearest land, within a short time the boats separated and were soon lost to sight of each other, they survived for up to nine days with little water. *"During the night of*

Wednesday -Thursday the wind dropped for a couple of hours and several showers of hail fell. The hailstones were eagerly scraped from our clothing and swallowed". Captain Benjamin Chave

Out of a total of one hundred and thirty-nine persons on board the 'Alnwick Castle', forty, including three of the crew of the 'Trevose', had died in the lifeboats through exposure, thirst and temporary madness brought on by drinking sea water. Two of the lifeboats were never seen or heard of again, Boson Whittaker was among the missing twenty one.

Southampton Hill, the old route out of the village to the West

Thomas Henry Wright

Service:	2nd Battalion Devonshire Regiment
Rank:	Private Service No.69064
Birth:	1899 Beauworth, Hampshire
Death:	31st May 1918 Bois de Buttes, France
Home Address:	Rockstone Cottages, East Street, Titchfield
Next of Kin:	George & Ellen Wright (nee Lillywhite)

Thomas was one of seven children, growing up in Titchfield, the son of a domestic gardener. He had also made horticulture his profession before joining the war in October 1915 by lying about his age on his enlistment papers, he was just 16.

On the 26th May 1918 two German prisoners of war confirmed, after interrogation, that a German attack by thirty- five divisions was to take place early the following morning.

As part of the 8th Division, 23rd Brigade, The 2nd Devon's marched forward four and a half miles to Bois de Buttes, a lightly wooded twin crested sandstone hill about 100 feet high & 500 yards wide & arrived at midnight on the 26th/27th May.

Thankfully they were able to use dugouts built for previous battles, as there was little time before the enemy started bombarding all positions with 6,000 trench mortars. The Devons were subjected to a ten minute bombardment of extremely effective gas followed by all available guns directed on to Bois des Buttes Buttes of a magnitude not previously experienced.

By 0930 hours the 50 survivors of the battalion divided into two groups and moved from the hill down to the road to engage the advancing Germans. Short of ammunition and greatly outnumbered, the survivors conducted a fighting withdrawal to the river. Lt Col Anderson-Morshead explained to the soldiers in the following words

"Your job for England, men, is to hold the blighters up as much as you can, to give our troops a chance on the other side of the river. There is no hope of relief we have to fight to the last."

The battalion significantly delayed the German advance, giving the French and British time to amass defences that finally brought a halt to the German advance. A total of 552 members of the 2nd Battalion, the Devonshire Regiment, were killed or captured that morning. Between 40 and 80 survivors managed to rejoin the retreating British forces.

The 2nd Devonshire Regiment were the first British unit to be honoured with the French Croix de Guerre in recognition of the actions performed on 27th May 1918, the first day of the Third Battle of the Aisne. Thomas Wright died of his injuries a few days later and his is one of the small number of identified graves at the Commonwealth Cemetery at Jonchery-Sur Vesle, near Reims.

French Croix de Guerre with palm

Titchfield Remembers Project

East Street showing a shop front and Rockstone Cottages on the right

Postscript

During our research we came across many stories of the servicemen who came home to Titchfield and carried on with their lives and it was our intention to include them in this book. However it soon became obvious that there were too many for this project to research. So their stories and photographs are featured on our website:

www.titchfieldremembers.co.uk.

Of the survivors, there were some who made it through the war, only to die in the following year from one of the worst strains of influenza the world has experienced. The Gamblins were one of the most unlucky families, not only losing two sons on active service, but a further three from influenza. The remaining son Frederick lived until he was 80.

Between 1919 and 1925 the numbers of young adult men dying were double that of women, as returning servicemen were particularly vulnerable to infection. Their health had been greatly impaired by four years of poor diet, damp and disease ridden billets, of physical wounds, the effects of gas or psychological illness. In addition to influenza, tuberculosis was another killer of ex servicemen, whose lives were cut short, but received no official recognition of their sacrifice. There are men on the Roll of Honour, identified as having survived the war, but many did not see their 30th birthday.

Some Titchfield servicemen who survived the war, such as the Hurden brothers and Herbert Laxton, have already had their stories written in local books. Another survivor Sapper Walter John Swatton whose family home was The West End Inn, West Street enlisted in the Royal Field Artillery in 1914. He showed incredible bravery and was awarded the Military Medal before swapping to the Royal Engineers in 1917. That year he then went behind enemy lines to mend a communication cable, for which he was awarded the Croix de Guerre. Walter died in 1973.

Sapper Walter Swatton circa 1914

At the end of 1918 in towns and villages across the country, Rolls of Honour were being written and decisions made on the best way to commemorate and remember the dead.

At a meeting of the Titchfield Parish Council on 3rd January 1919 it was decided to *'call a public meeting to discuss and appoint a committee to determine what course should be adopted in erecting a war memorial....... That a meeting be called for Thursday January 16th at 8pm.'* The next parish meeting discussed *'entertainment for those who have served'* and the outcome of that discussion was the celebration on 23rd July 1919. Among those who came home to celebrate were William Bowman, Harry Simeton, Arthur Bedford and Harry Childs. Their faces and stories are amongst a dozen or more on the Titchfield Remembers website.

In July 1920, the Titchfield Memorial was installed in the grounds of the Parish Rooms and the unveiling ceremony took place.

The First World War had a devastating impact on small villages like Titchfield, where so many young men should have come back and continued their role in village life.

We have felt honoured to have been able to tell their stories as our tribute to their sacrifice.

> "All we have of freedom, all we use or know
> This our fathers bought for us long and long ago."
>
> *(Rudyard Kipling)*

Beyond the Memorial

On Sunday 19th July 1919 London unveiled the Cenotaph and the following Wednesday Titchfield had its big peace celebration

July 1920 A solemn occasion overlooked by the houses associated with Charlie Chalk and Frederick Leat

Appendix

Sources

Commonwealth War Graves Commission - www.cwgc.org

Ancestry - www.ancestry.com

Genes Reunited - www.genesreunited.co.uk

British Red Cross - www.redcross.org.uk

Hampshire War Memorials - www.hampshirewarmemorials.com

Royal Hampshire Regimental Museum - serleshouse.co.uk

Royal Artillery Library Woolwich - firepower.org.uk

Metropolitan & City Police Orphans Fund - www.met-cityorphans.org.uk

Malvern College - www.malverncollege.org.uk

The Soldier in later Medieval England: AHRC research project - www.medievalsoldier.org

Isle of Wight Memorials - www.isle-of-wight-memorials.org.uk

Soldiers & Soldiering in Britain 1750-1810 - www.arts.leeds.ac.uk/redcoats/

South African Military History Society - http://samilitaryhistory.org/vol061sm.html

BBC Voices of the First World War series - http://www.bbc.co.uk/programmes/b03t7p9l

Prisoners of the First World War ICRC historical archives - www.grandeguerre.icrc.org

The Biscuit Boys - http://www.purley.eu/RBR3242.pdf

National Army Museum - www.nam.ac.uk

Canadian Expeditionary Force Study Group - http://cefresearch.ca

Infectious Diseases in History - http://urbanrim.org.uk

Army structure - www.britisharmedforces.org

Naval History explained - www.naval-history.net

General WWI - www.longlongtrail.co.uk

Multimedia History of World War One - www.firstworldwar.com

Portsmouth Pals - www.pompeypals.org.uk

London Gazette - www.thegazette.co.uk

Early Newspapers - www.britishnewspaperarchive.co.uk

Missing Soldiers - www.fromellesdiscussiongroup.com

Berkshire & Wiltshire Regiments - www.thewardrobe.org.uk

The British Postal Museum - www.postalheritage.org.uk

Royal Victoria Hospital and Military Cemetery Netley - www.netley-military-cemetery.co.uk

15th Hampshires - www.plugstreet-archaeology.com

Beyond the Memorial

Titchfield Street Maps 1911

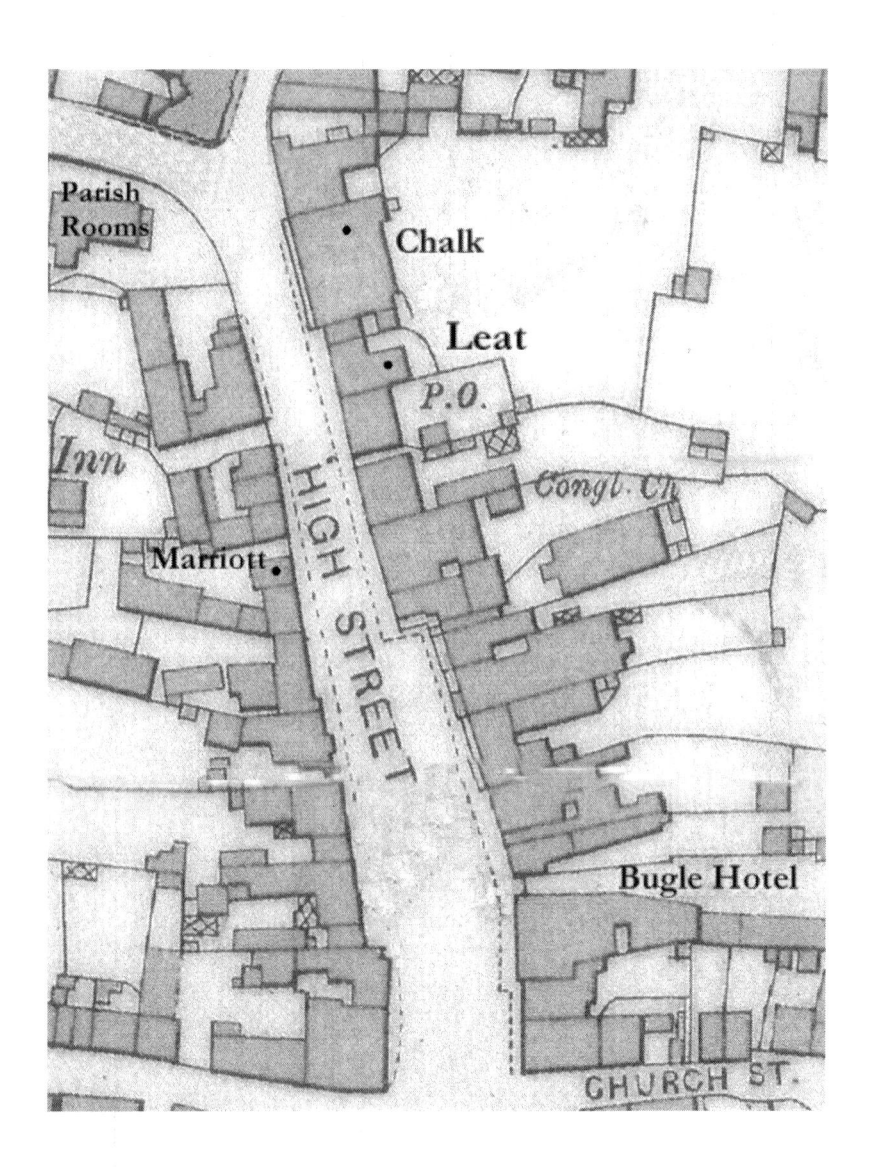

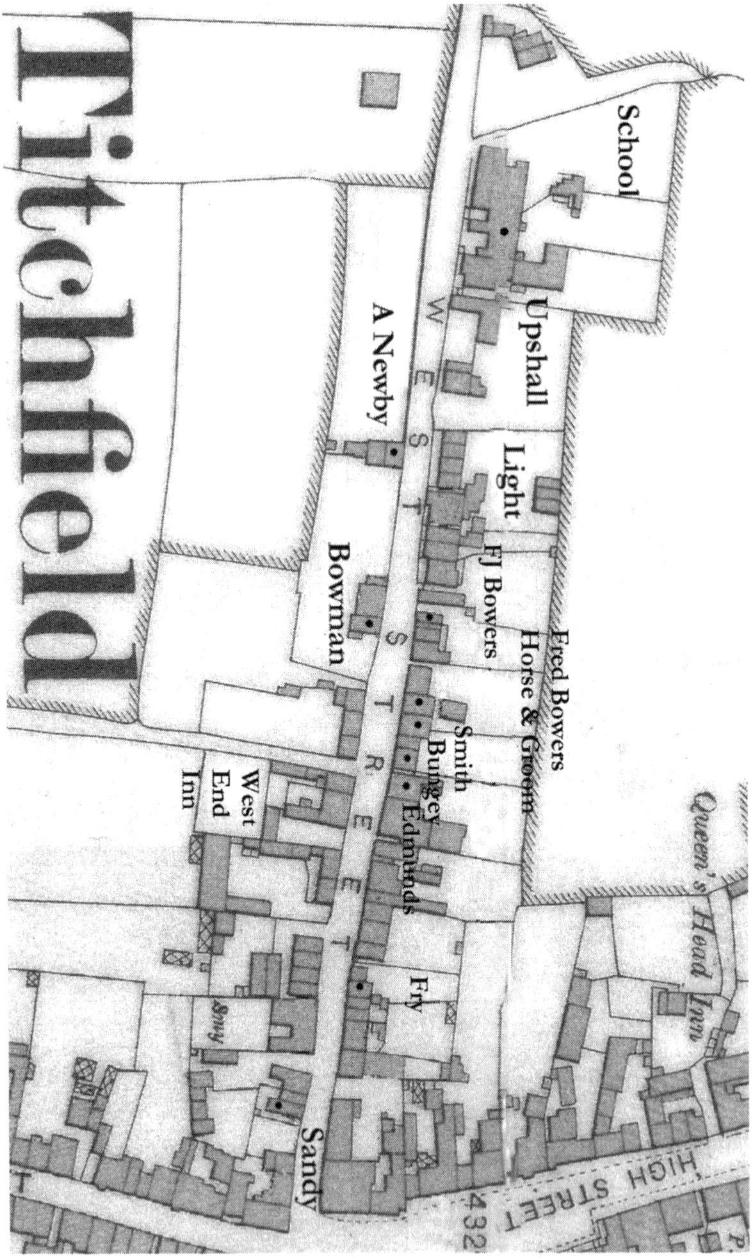
Titchfield
School
Upshall
A Newby
Light
FJ Bowers
Fred Bowers
Horse & Groom
Bowman
Smith
Bungey
Edmunds
West End Inn
Fry
Sandy
WEST STREET
Queen's Head Inn
HIGH STREET
432

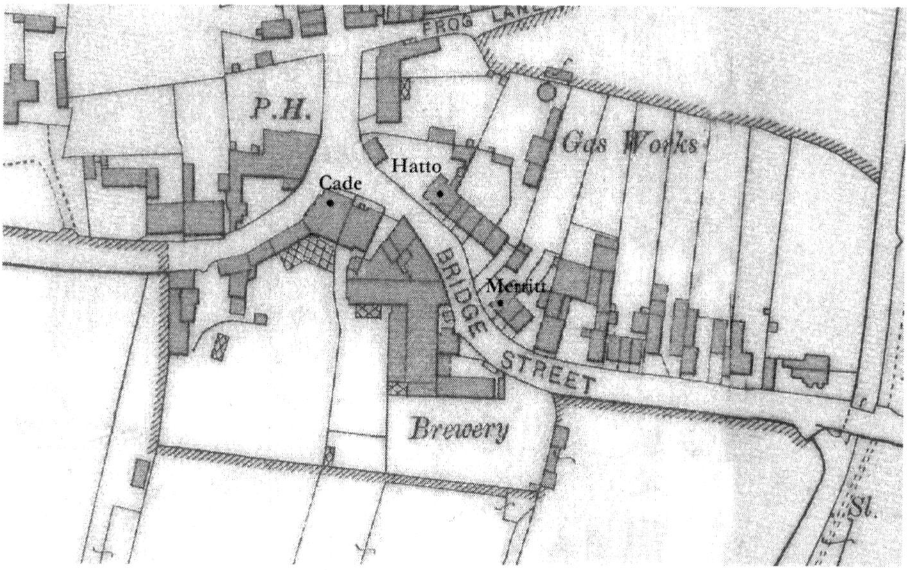
FROG LANE
P.H.
Gas Works
Hatto
Cade
BRIDGE ST.
Merritt
STREET
Brewery
St.

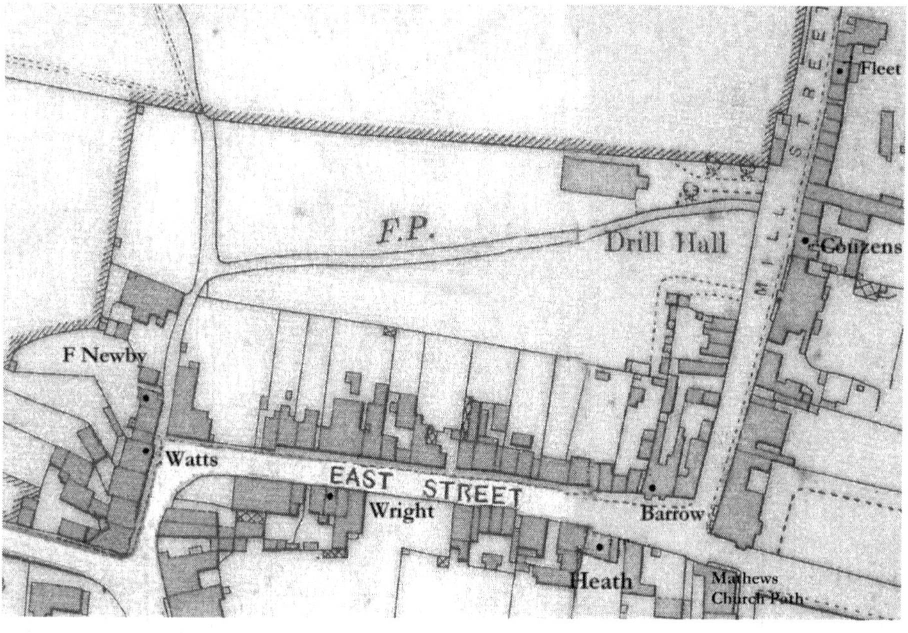
Fleet
MILL STREET
F.P.
Drill Hall
Couzens
F Newby
Watts
EAST STREET
Wright
Barrow
Heath
Mathews
Church Path

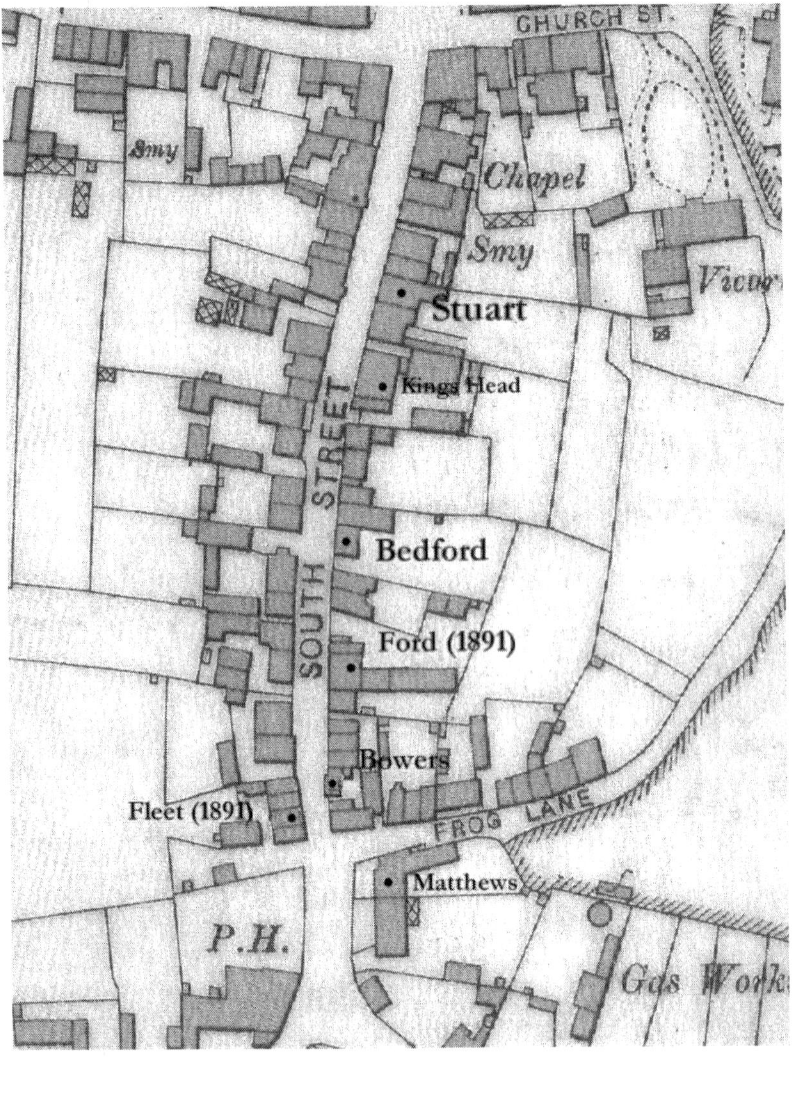
CHURCH ST.
Smy
Chapel
Smy
Vicar
Stuart
Kings Head
SOUTH STREET
Bedford
Ford (1891)
Bowers
Fleet (1891)
FROG LANE
Matthews
P.H.
Gas Work

Titchfield Roll of Honour

with amendments made 2016

This Book is Dedicated to the Men of the Ancient Parish of Titchfield, Hampshire who to their Honour answered the Call of King and Country and Ventured their Lives in the Great War of 1914 - 1918
And in Grateful Memory of those who made the Supreme Sacrifice
G Stanley Morley Vicar, Charles H Ransome, Arthur E Mason Wardens

Numbers denote page in book
Memorial names in bold
Mistakes in italics

1	F A L Andrews		Captain RN		RAMC
1	Alfred Avey		RFA?	2	John H Bowers
1	Herbert Avey		RMSF?	2	William Bowes	RIP
1	Walter Avey		6th Hants	2	Charles Bowman	6th Hants
1	Archibald H Bailey		HMS Victory	2	Harry Bowman	14th Hants
1	Charles Barton		6th Hants	2	Harry Bowman	GOC
1	George Barton		HMS Britannia	2	James Bowman	GOC
1	Robert Barton		2nd Hants	2	Mark Bowman	HMS Birmingham
1	Arthur Bedford		HMS Hyacinth	2	Sidney Bowman	1st Hants
1	Albert Bedford		HMS Glory	3	William Bowman	GOC
1	George W Bedford	RIP	1st East Yorks	3	William Bowman	3rd Hants
1	Sidney C Bedford		5th Hants	3	George Bowen	14th Hants
1	William Benham		3rd Hants	3	Sidney S Bretherton	D C LI
1	Frank Bennett		1th Hants	3	Frederick J Bustow	Wessex
1	Albert Biddle	RIP	2nd Kings Royal Rifles	3	Frederick Bryant	
1	Frank Biddle	RIP	10th Hants	3	Herbert Bungey	3rd Wiltshires	RIP
2	Ernest Bower		1st Hants	3	David Burgess	AOE?
2	Charles J Bowers		RGA	3	Harry Burgess	7th Wellington Inf
2	Ernest Bowers		ASC?	3	William Henry Burgess	1st/6th Hants
2	Frederick J Bowers	RIP	14th Hants	3	William Burgess	6th Hants
2	Frederick J Bowers	RIP	RFA	3	William G Burgess	3rd Hants
2	Fred Bowers		10th Hants	3	Charles Butcher/Burgess	R M L I
2	Harry Bowers			3	Harry Butcher	R M L I
2	Harry W Bowers	RIP	(Serg) 15th Hants	3	John Butcher	R M L I
				3	Francis T D Cade	(Capt) 11th Hants	RIP

4	Thomas Carr?		HMS Achilles		6	William E Fielding	14th Hants	
4	Charlie Chalk		Australian Inf	RIP	6	John Fleet (L. Corp)	14th Hants	RIP
4	Frederick G Chant		HMS Amazon		6	George Ford	HMS Good Hope	RIP
4	Frederick J Clark		HMS Vincent		6	William Gamblin	2nd Hants	
4	William B Clark		Coastguard		6	Richard Gibbons (Lieut)	6th Hants	
4	William E Clark (juno)		HMS Monarch		7	William F Goddard	3rd Hants	
4	Arthur E Collins		East Lancs		7	Frank Gough	Hants Carabineers?	
4	John Collins		HMS prince of Wales		7	Frederick Gray	3rd Hants	
4	Leonard Conway		HMS Irresistable		7	Thomas Gregory	RN (Stoker PO)	
4	Harry F Compton		HMS Feadros		7	John J Hacker	R F A	
4	Arthur Couzens		HMS Submarine		7	Thomas Haggard	3rd Hants	
4	Edward Couzens		10th Hants		7	Caleb Hales	2nd Hants	
4	Harry Couzens		7th Hants	RIP	7	Harry Hales	HMS King Edward VII	
4	Allan E Cross		R M G		7	William Hatto	(Serg)1st Hants	RIP
4	Rupert A Cross		R E		7	Charles F Heath	2nd Hants	
5	Rex Curtis Captain		6th Hants		7	Edward Heath	RGA	
5	Alfred Downer		RHA		7	Edward Heath	RGA	
5	Sidney F Downes		Somerset L I		7	Ernest Heath	(Serg)GVC	RIP
5	Henry Edmunds		(Corp) 14th Hants	RIP	7	William F Heath	2nd Hants	
5	Oliver Edmunds		16th Hants		7	Frederick Howard	RFA	
5	William Edwards		RFC		7	Hensley Hurdon	HMS Princess Royal	
5	Percy Elms		RAMC		8	Oliver Hurden	HMS Agincourt	
5	Albert W Evans		2nd Hants		8	Willoughby Hurden	HMS Princess Royal	
5	Algernon Evans		GOC		8	Frank Isaacs	AOE	
5	Herbert Eyes		6th Hants		8	Fred Jones	AOE	
5	Sidney Eyers		6th Hants		8	George Kinch	HMS Agincourt	
5	Cyril H Fay				8	Charles King	1st Hants	
5	Arthur Fearne		(Serg) 6th Hants	RIP	8	Edward Lamb	HMS Assistance	
5	Harry Feins		HMS Rattlesnake		8	Harry Lambert	HMLS	
5	Frank Fielder		6th Hants		8	Herbert Loxton	RGA	
5	Gerald Fielder		Beds Yeomanry		8	Frederick C Leat	HMS Queen Mary	RIP
6	Grover Fielder		RHA		8	Albert E Lee	13th Hants	
6	Harry Fielder		HMS Minotaur		8	John Lee	RHG	

	Name	Unit		Name	Unit	
8	Willis Lee	Dorset	10	Harry Newby	12th Lancers	
8	Arthur Light	Hants	10	Albert Oaks	RGA	
8	Ernest Light	15th Hants	RIP	11	Thomas Oaks	Navy Brigade
8	Frank Light	3rd Hants	11	Albert Oakshott	6th Hants	
9	James Light	1st Hants	11	Sidney Oakshott	NZ Contigent	
9	John Light	RGA	11	F Orange-Bromhead	R E (Lieut)	
9	A Lock	6th Hants	11	John Orange-Bromhead	Yorks L I (Lieut)	
9	Charles W Long	RGA	11	Frederick F Pack	1st Hants	
9	Harry F Long	RGA	11	Thomas Pack	Dorset	
9	John Long	RGA	11	Harrington Owen Parr	7th Rajputs (Lieut Col)	
9	Arthur Long	HMS Agincourt	11	Andrew Pharoah	R A M C	
9	Arthur E Mason	6th Hants	11	Ernest Pharoah	RGA	RIP
9	Alfred F Matthews	2nd Hants	11	W Pharoah	Hants Carabineers	
9	Charles E Matthews	5th Rifle Brig	11	Duncan Phelps	(2nd Lieut) Sussex	RIP
9	Frederick G Matthews	Dorsets	11	Arthur W Phillimore	1st Hants	
9	George Matthews	1st Hants	11	George Powell	Hants Carabineers	
9	Harry G Matthews	H M Submarine E G	11	George G Powell	R E	
9	Leonard E Matthews	R E	11	Reginald G Powell	3rd Canadians	
9	William J Matthews	RGA	12	John Price	7th Border Reg	RIP
10	William Matthews	(Corp) 14th Hants	RIP	12	Thomas Price	6th Hants
10	William T Matthews	HMS Neptune	12	Robert H Randall	6th Queens Royals (WS)	
10	David McEvely	HMS Neptune	12	Basil Read	HMS Fenders	
10	John McEvely	HMS Hercules	12	Henry Read	7th Hants	
10	Percy G Merritt	HM Submarine	RIP	12	Charles Redman	HMS King George V
10	Richard F Merritt	15th Hants	12	Owen Roberts	RE	
10	Albert Mondey	HMS Princess Royal	12	John Roxburgh	RGA	
10	John Mondey	HMS Boyne	12	John Sandy	Wessex	
10	G Stanley Morley	6th Hants RAMC	12	Thomas Sandy	GOC	
10	Arthur Newby	15th Hants	RIP	12	William Sandy	2nd Hants	RIP
10	Charles Newby	6th Hants	12	Thomas Sapsard	6th Hants	
10	Edgar Newby	1st Hants	12	Ernest Sanders	Hants Carabineers	
10	Frederick Newby	1st Hants	RIP	12	Charles Scammel	Grenadiers	
10	Frank Newby	Dorset	12	Thomas Shawyer	HMS Hogue	

12	John Sims	HMS Cressy	RIP	15	Charles E West	?	
13	Thomas Sims	HMS Agincourt		15	Frank West	Mech Trans Corps	
13	Albert Smith	10th Hants	RIP	15	Frederick West	HMS King Edward VII	
13	Albert Smith	10th Hants		15	Walter West	?	
13	Bertie Smith	6th Hants		15	Richard C Welman	GOC	
13	David Smith	HMS Snodgard		15	Charles Whitear	HMS Leviathan?	
13	Frank Smith	2nd Hants		15	Charles G Whitear	GOC	
13	Frank Smith	10th Hants	RIP	15	Frederick Whitear	GOC	
13	Harold Smith	Hants Carabineers		15	Harold Whitear	RFA	
13	James Smith	A O C		15	Henry Whitear	RFA	
13	Leonard Smith	10th Hants		15	John Whitear	HMS Unity	
13	Walter Smith	R G V C	RIP	15	Carnavon L Whittacker	Merchantile Marine	RIP
13	William Smith	Dragoon Guards		15	Arthur C Whittacker	Hants Yeomanry	RIP
13	Herbert J R Spurgin	10th Hants		15	Ernest Williams	R F A	
13	Spurgin	10th Hants		15	Richard Williams	GSC	
13	Strude	HMS Glasgow		15	Henry F Winter	?	
13	Frank Stuart	1st DCLI	RIP	16	George M Wright	R A M C	RIP
14	Charles Swatton	RGA		16	Thomas Wright	2nd Devons	
14	Harry Swatton	10th Hants *did not die?*	RIP				
14	Walter Swatton	RFA			Cpl. R Marriott (missed of)	R.E.	RIP
14	John Taylor	3rd Hants					
14	Victor Taylor (Corp)	2nd Royal Berks	RIP				
14	James Tremlett	Hants Carabineers					
14	Alfred E Tucker	5th Hants					
14	John Tucker	R M L F					
14	Ernest Turner	R E					
14	Alexander W Twynham	A S C					
14	Donald Upshall	Northbld Fus	RIP				
14	Bertie Watkins	2nd Hants					
14	Frank Watkins	RFA					
14	Sidney Watkins	RFA					
14	Ernest C Watts	6th Hants					
14	Francis C Watts	HMS Black Prince	RIP				